Space, Time and Crisis:

The Theatre of René Marqués

Space, Time and Crisis:
The Theatre of René Marqués

by

Bonnie Hildebrand Reynolds

Spanish Literature Publishing Company
York, South Carolina
1988

Library of Congress Catalog Card Number 87-61514

ISBN 0-938972-13-8

Printed in the United States of America

To my parents, Florence and Marshall Hildebrand, my husband Bob, my children, Lisa and Mike, and my Puerto Rican brother and sister, Joe and Maggie Lacomba, gracious loving people all.

Mataréis al Dios del Miedo y
sólo entonces seréis libres.

René Marqués

Contents

Preface

René Marqués' total writings cover novel, short story and essay, but it is his theatre which brought him international recognition and gave him a place among the great Latin American dramatists of the Twentieth Century. The acclaim which the author has received for his dramatic works is the result of his expert handling of regional thematic concerns on a universal level as well as of the ways in which he incorporated and experimented with state-of-the-art techniques. The following is an in-depth study of both the thematic and technical aspects of his theatre and includes discussion of one unpublished work (*Los condenados*) and two which have never been produced (*David y Jonatán* and *Tito y Berenice*).

Although there do exist two book-length publications on the total body of Marqués' literary works (Pilditch. *René Marqués, A Study of His Fiction;* Martin. *René Marqués*), neither treats the plays within the perspective of the theatre nor do they attempt to place the dramatist in the scheme of Latin American drama of this century. In addition to the two books, there are numerous published articles dealing with selected plays, as well as various master's theses and doctoral dissertations. I refer the reader to three excellent bibliographical sources for a complete listing of these studies: Leon F. Lyday and George W. Woodyard's *A Bibliography of Latin American Theatre Criticism: 1940-1970;* Esther Rodriguez Ramos' "Aproximación a una bibliografía: René Marqués," in *Sin Nombre*, Vol. X, No. 3 (oct-nov 1979); and Nilda González' *Bibliografía de Teatro Puertorriqueño (Siglos XIX y XX)*.

My intent in this book is first to place René Marqués within the historical background of not only Puerto Rican theatre, but Latin American theatre as well. The main body is then devoted to analyses of the published and/or produced plays. The methodology which I have followed is based mainly upon the author's use of space and time. From there my analyses branch out into what I believe is a more holistic approach to Marqués' theatre than has been taken in other studies. The theorists upon whom I depend vary according to the demands of each individual work. However, in my own preparation, I have been influenced by the writings of dramatic theorist J. L. Styan and philosopher Susanne Langer, both of whose perceptive statements about space and time in the theatre are valid in relation to René Marqués' works in particular.

Since Marqués' various styles did not develop chronologically but rather simultaneously, I do not necessarily analyze the works in the order in which they were written. Rather, I have grouped the plays in ways meaningful to the author's use of space and time as well as to the varied and rich styles which he employed.

I wish to thank two very special people who have helped in this study in many invaluable ways. I, however, am solely responsible for any flaws or deficiencies to be found. A warm thank-you goes to my good friend and colleague, George W. Woodyard, editor of the *Latin American Theatre Review*, for his encouragement and suggestions along the way, and for making available to me the journal's extensive library. A most special thanks goes to my friend, José M. Lacomba, who has encouraged and advised me extensively on the research and the writing of the manuscript while at the same time he has taught me about the beautiful people and the land of Puerto Rico. The research was initially supported by grants from the National Endowment for the Humanities and the Commission on Academic Excellence at the University of Louisville.

Chapter I

Puerto Rican Theatre in Its Spanish American Context .

In 1938, don Emilio Belaval, at that time the president of the Puerto Rican Atheneum, delivered his famous talk entitled "Lo que podría ser un teatro puertorriqueño," a talk which, together with the subsequent establishment of the theatre group *Areyto,* has been considered the motivating force in the development of Puerto Rican theatre in the Twentieth Century. Mr. Belaval said: "Algún día de estos tendremos que unirnos para crear un gran teatro nuestro, donde todo nos pertenezca: el tema, el actor, los motivos decorativos, las ideas, la estética" (Belaval in *Areyto Mayor* 245). Whether the venerable don Emilio knew it or not, his words and his actions were echoes of those heard throughout Spanish America. In fact, the history of the theatre in Puerto Rico up to the present reflects and is part of the history of the theatre in Spanish America.

It is a theatre which has developed according to the prevailing political and cultural circumstances of the Spanish colonies, who for centuries suffered the official censorship of the Church and of the government. Today, with the exception of Puerto Rico, those colonies are autonomous nations, but their theatre continues to suffer censorship of one kind or another. At the same time, it is a theatre which in the present has derived stylistically from the major trends of the century, combining these with thematics based on the social and political conditions that exist in the diverse Hispanic regions of America. An inventory of the history of the theatre in Spanish America reveals that Puerto Rico has nearly always followed the same route as its Hispanic neighbors. In the present century its own theatre, of high quality, has strong Hispanic and American resonances. Because of its marginal political and economic position among the Spanish colonies, the Island followed a few steps behind. Puerto Rico now can take pride in having in force a theatre that shares imilar history, problems and triumphs with the regions of America that began as Spanish colonies.

In the Spanish American theatre of the Twentieth Century, we can perceive the development of a theatrical consciousness free of the traditional Spanish model, in which the dramatists utilize and are inspired by the new methods that appeared in Europe at the early part of the century. Characteristically, they employ the new methodologies in combination with themes relevant to the unique situations of the various regions. In an era of advanced technology and better methods of communication, the Spanish Americans broke their literary bonds with Spain and began to look for new directions. The techniques and theories of the Europeans George Bernard Shaw, Luigi Pirandello, Bertolt Brecht, Samuel Beckett, Eugene Ionesco, Jean Genet and Antonin Artaud, as well as those of the North Americans Eugene O'Neill and Tennessee Williams, have served as models for the Spanish American stage. On the other hand, the new century has seen the formation of several theatrical groups, the establishment of theatre departments and institutes in the principal universities, and the organization of theatre festivals in many of the major cities.

Professor Frank Dauster, in his *Historia del teatro hispanoamericano: Siglos XIX-XX*, shows us the unified character of the theatre in the Spanish American regions:

> A pesar de las fronteras políticas y del precario nivel cultural, causas de que muchos países no sepan lo que ocurre en otros, el proceso cultural hispanoamericano es uno, con el natural colorido regional ocasionado por la peculiar fisonomía política, étnica e histórica de cada nación o región. (25)

According to Dauster, the similarities evident in almost all of the regions occur in three periods that, while not simultaneous, are harmonious in the creative process. At the beginning of this century, with the exception of some works from the Rio de la Plata area such as Florencio Sánchez's *Barranca abajo*, the theatre followed for the most part the examples set by Spain. Until the end of the 1920's, its development was at a standstill. At that time there appeared a fondness for experimentation, especially evident in groups whose goals were the total renovation of the theatre. This tendency, according to Dauster, appears in Mexico in 1928 with the *Grupo Ulises*, in Cuba with the efforts prior to the formation of the *Teatro de la Cueva* in 1928; in the Rio de la Plata with the *Teatro del Pueblo* in 1930; and in Puerto Rico between the years 1938-41 with the Atheneum's theatre contest in 1938 and the establishment of the *Grupo Areyto* in 1940-41.

The third period which Dauster mentions is the present which he calls the period of "pleno florecimiento." In this period, according to him, "apenas hay país que no tenga valiosos dramaturgos, que no despliegue alguna actividad teatral de categoría, que no esté en fin produciendo más y mejor teatro que en cualquier momento de su historia" (26). Presently, not only is there much theatrical activity within the different countries and regions, but also there is a cultural exchange among the dramatists, directors, and actors, especially by means of international festivals and the several journals devoted exclusively to Latin American theatre; in particular: *Conjunto, Latin American Theatre Review, Tramoya, Intermedio de Puerto Rico,* and the CELCIT publications.

In Puerto Rico during the first third of the century, works of an impressive variety were written. Angelina Morfi, who has classified the works of this period, informs us that: "Simultáneamente se escribe teatro de sátira política, de orientación obrera, de evocación histórica, de crítica de costumbres y comedia de salón" (234). Obviously, there was interest in producing theatre in Puerto Rico during this period but there was lacking a unified purpose, artistic preparation and, as always, money to create a body of meritorious works. In 1933, several theatre groups came together in the *Club Artístico del Casino de Puerto Rico* (Belaval, *El Mundo,* 14). During its five years of life the Artistic Club produced one play a week, several of which were the works of Puerto Rican authors, although the Spanish influence still permeated their creations. Emilio Belaval himself pointed out in an article commemorating the first season of the Annual Theatre Festival of the Puerto Rican Culture Institute:

> Cuando en el 1936 [sic] yo pronuncié en el Ateneo Puertorriqueño una conferencia sobre "Lo que podría ser un Teatro Puertorriqueño" como algo distinto a lo que se entendía por dicho teatro, un teatro que recogiera tanto las esencias populares de nuestro ancestro dramático español como las esencias culturales de nuestro europeísmo circulante, disfruté por un tiempo de una profunda impopularidad en los círculos teatrales de Puerto Rico. Nadie intuía la posibilidad que pudiera existir una temática, un estilo de actuación, una escenografía puertorriqueños, fuera de los moldes y modos del Teatro Español. (*El Mundo* 17 de marzo de 1958)

When, in 1938, the Casino withdrew from sponsorship of the theatre, it was only natural that the group of theatre lovers would seek refuge in the Atheneum, considering that Belaval was then president of that institution.

Even though the Puerto Rican Atheneum had not demonstrated loyalty to the theatre before that year, there were historical
antecedents for the support of such activity. According to Josefina
Rivera de Alvarez and Nilda González, the Atheneum awarded a
theatre prize in 1913 to Matías González García for the work *Gritos de
angustia* (González 167; Rivera 702); and two years later, in 1915, a
prize was awarded for *Los primeros fríos*, the work of José Pérez Losada,
a Spaniard permanently residing in Puerto Rico, who did much to
encourage the writing and production of theatre in the early years of
the century (González 167; Rivera 1183). A minuscule examination of
the official minutes of the Atheneum reveals no other theatre competition until 1928, when, as part of the Interantillean Contest, the
following plays received prizes:

> *Juan Ponce de León* by José Ramírez Santibáñez y Carlos N. Carreras;
> *Por mi tierra y por mi dama* by Matías González García;
> *Cuando termine el amor* by Miguel Angel Yumet. (*Actas* Vol. 7)

With these historidal antecedents, and following Belaval's
leadership, the Atheneum once again promoted the theatre when, in
1938, it sponsored a one-week course on theatre that included the
following lectures:

1. "Lo que podría ser un teatro puertorriqueño," el Lcdo. Emilio S.
   Belaval (lunes, el 20 de junio);
2. "Canteras artísticas de nuestro teatro," don Francisco Manrique
   Cabrera (martes, el 21 de junio);
3. "El teatro del puertorriqueño Tapia," don Manuel García Díaz
   (miércoles, el 22 de junio);
4. "El teatro del puertorriqueño Brau," doña Antonia Sáez (jueves, el
   23 de junio);
5. "Vida y pasión de la danza puertorriqueña," don Augusto A.
   Rodríguez (viernes, el 24 de junio). (*Actas*, Vol. 8, 127)

That same year, the Atheneum sponsored a Puerto Rican theatre
contest and awarded the following prizes:

> Premio: *El clamor de los surcos* by don Manual Méndez Ballester;
> Mención Honorífica: *Esta noche jueqa el Jóker* by Fernando Sierra
> Berdecía;
> Mención: *Desmonte* by Gonzalo A. del Toro. (*Actas*, Vol. 8 128)

Subsequently, the Puerto Rican Atheneum sponsored the production of Sierra Berdecía's work, *Esta noche jueqa el Jóker*, and Méndez Ballester's *El clamor de los surcos*.

At the request of don Géigel Polanco, in 1939, Emilio Belaval, as president of the Atheneum, prepared a plan of development of Puerto Rican theatre. This encouraged Belaval to create the famous group *Areyto* which, in a short life of only one year produced four Puerto Rican works and served as the driving force into the following decades. During the 1940's, as a result of so much theatrical activity, other groups appeared, such as *Tinglado Puertorriqueño* (1945), of Francisco Arriví, and *Teatro Nuestro* (1949), of René Marqués.

With the establishment of the *Teatro Experimental* in 1951, the Puerto Rican Atheneum once again demonstrated its decisive leadership in the encouragement of theatrical art on the Island. René Marqués, who was secretary of the Atheneum's governing board in that year, proposed the idea to the Board. He is now known as cofounder of the *Teatro Experimental*, together with José M. Lacomba. On May 19, 1952, Marqués made public in *El Mundo* the following reasons for the establishment of the theatre: "El Teatro Experimental del Ateneo es una organización del Ateneo para el fomento y el cultivo del teatro. Tiene dos objetivos fundamentales: El primero es dar a conocer obras extranjeras o puertorriqueñas que por su carácter no serían producidas por el teatro comercial. El segundo es poner el teatro al alcance de todo el pueblo bajando los precios de entrada a un mínimo" (13). Since no Puerto Rican work was submitted, the Experimental Theatre's productions began with a foreign work, Albert Camus' *Le malentendu*, which was followed by other works from the contemporary European stage.

The impulse which determined the future of the theatre in Puerto Rico erupted with the production in 1953-54 of Marqués' own *La carreta*, on the stage of the *Teatro Experimental* in the Atheneum. Such was the production's success that Marqués and his group of actors took the play to the Tapia Theatre which could accommodate a larger audience than could the Atheneum's smaller theatre. The developing interest in producing works by Puerto Ricans, with Puerto Rican themes, led to the establishment of the annual Puerto Rican Theatre Festivals which the Puerto Rican Culture Institute has sponsored since 1958.

René Marqués is the author who contributed most to the encouragement of theatrical activity in present-day Puerto Rico. Through his own energy and perseverance he was influential not only in creating an interest in high quality theatre by Puerto Rican authors, but also he was responsible for staging such works. All of his own dramas project the conflictive politico-cultural reality of the island to a universal level, always experimenting with and developing new and interesting techniques unknown before on the Island's few stages. In this way, besides presenting the specific and detailed problems inherent in a colonial society, he proposed to define the identity of the Puerto Rican in the contemporary world.

Chapter II

Genesis of Styles

René Marqués, the dramatist, received numerous prizes and recognitions for his theatrical works. His major dramas have been translated into several languages and presented in various countries. Luis Rafael Sánchez appropriately claims in the article "Cinco problemas al escritor puertorriqueno" (120): "Una obra artística no es mejor ni peor porque su intención política sea noble o responsable." Rather, he contends, in order to endure, a literary work must demonstrate an esthetic of the highest quality. Marqués' works owe their endurance and international acclaim to the author's ability to communicate universal aspects inherent in the unique cultural and political realities that he dramatized. Marqués' technical mastery of contemporary theatrical recourses placed him at the leading edge among the Spanish American playwrights of his day. In his major works, the harmonious balance he created between technique and thematic content reflects a similar equilibrium between the regional and universal levels of his dramas. Thus, was he able to attract the attention of such varied audiences.

For Marqués, time and space, always of utmost importance in the creation of any dramatic experience, are dynamic forces that serve to establish the balance between form and content in his works. The particular relationships established between these two forces in his dramas signal, for characters and spectators alike, the cultural-political crisis which is at the heart of Marqués' world view. In each circumstance, this relationship motivates a response on the part of the central characters, who are responsible for prolonging such crises because of their own inaction. Meanwhile, time moves inexorably forward, forcing them finally to make the choices they have previously avoided. Although one may not always agree with the outcome, the characters' final choice resolves their personal dramatic crises. Their final actions, however, do not necessarily resolve the crises on the universal level perceived by the spectator. Marqués' dramas often leave these universal crises unresolved so that the viewer must, in the end, make his/her own choice in order to preserve the play's equilibrium.)

Both technically and philosophically, Marqués' theatre reflects his interest in and knowledge of the most significant European and American writers of the period. The dramatist himself revealed his admiration for the Italian playwright Luigi Pirandello and the American Eugene O'Neill in two critical essays published in Puerto Rico ("Luigi Pirandello: El Hombre ante su Espejo" and "Reseña: O'Neill, Eugene. *A Moon for the Misbegotten*"); and the innovative theatrical concepts of these two authors are evident in Marqués' own technical approaches. In combination with his technical innovations, Marqués also demonstrates an affinity for the existential philosophers of his day, i.e. Albert Camus, Jean Paul Sartre, and Martin Heidegger. Technical innovations and an existentialist philosophy form the basis of Marqués' expression of his own strong commitment to the preservation of Puerto Rico's cultural identity, as well as the establishment of its political autonomy.

(Marqués' spatial and temporal realms are multidimensional in the sense that the identifiable units of space and time, as well as their relationships to one another act in concert to create the whole work. The created dimensions are of two kinds. One is related to what the spectator sees and perceives directly. The second category is comprised of the spatial and temporal dimensions that exist implicitly in the relationships within a specific work.)

Marqués' explicit temporal strategy includes both the actual playing time and the notion of chronological time within the play's events. The spectator is aware of this later ordering whether or not the work's various episodes are presented in a cause and effect fashion. Rhythm and tempo, concepts which according to J. L. Styan are necessary for a "satisfactory understanding of a play's orchestration" (10), operate implicitly with the more obvious temporal elements to create a sense of inner, psychological time. This later illusory time exists only during the play's staging and is synchronized with the real playing time and chronology of events.

(Explicit spatial dimensions are created by the stage set and include such elements as props, distances and levels, gestures, and the positions which the actors occupy at any given time. The implicit dimensions arise from all the play's elements working together, including the dialogue as well as costuming, sounds and the others already mentioned. For instance, the spectator may see a physical space resembling a living room such as in *Los soles truncos*. As the play progresses, however, an ambiance of entrapment, jealousy, and despair becomes an inseparable part of the physical space. At the end of the performance, the physical space remains unchanged. On the other hand, the ambiance ceases to exist until it is re-created in the next staging. During a performance, the physical space is transformed into an illusory one once the ambiance becomes an integral part of the stage set. This illusory space may be projected both outside of the physical limits of the stage and of the dramatized events, even transcending time if necessary to the communication system of a given play.

These various dimensions coexist in varying proportions in each of Marqués' dramas, creating a woven texture in the plays. In the weaving, dramatic crises are born that on the surface are all quite different from one another, but in a more profound way, always point to the conflict at the heart of René Marqués' Puerto Rican circumstance and world view.

The varied and rich theatrical techniques which Marqués employs enhance the woven quality of the spatial and temporal aspects, often serve to intensify the ambiance created in each work, and always emphasize some aspect of space or time on one or more of a work's levels. The major reappearing recourses are of two categories: auditory signals (voices from off stage, music, birds, etc.), and visual signals (characters crossing the stage with no dialogue, empty stages, lighting and darkening of the stage while events are reported auditorily, the symbolic use of colors, etc.). These paticular techniques can be related to Marqués' interest in the theatre of Eugene O'Neill and most certainly to his own studies at Columbia University and in Erwin Piscator's Dramatic Workshop in New York during 1949.

In varying degrees, Marqués imposes the following focuses on his dramatic works: the coetaneous and contiguous possibilities of time and space, especially seen in *Los soles truncos* and *Un niño azul para esa sombra*; the relationship between dramatic rhythm and the creation of virtual space such as in *La carreta* and *Carnaval afuera, carnaval adentro*; re-constructed history as a means of seeing the future, especially apparent in *La muerte no entrará en palacio* and *Mariana o el alba*; entrapment in a meaningless world with a Sartrean "no exit" such as in *El apartamiento* and *La casa sin reloj*; and the overt creation of a cinematic celerity whose purpose is to reveal the eternal existence of time and power as forces that destroy man's ability to love, made most clear in his so-called Biblical plays, *Sacrificio en el Monte Moriah* and *David y Jonatán/Tito y Berenice*.

A brief look at Marqués' earliest plays shows each of these approaches to have been present from his earliest incursions into drama. Throughout the twenty years that he wrote, he refined and intensified the various techniques and focuses with which he began his work, always with the goal of expressing his own personal commitment to the development of his beloved Puerto Rico's fullest potential.

El hombre y sus sueños is Marqués' earliest dramatic work. The play was written in 1948 and published that same year in *Asomante*. Not until May, 1971, did it appear on stage, however. The subtitle, "Esbozo intrascendente para un drama trascendental" structures the play thematically and gives us insight into the larger structures of Marqués' later works. The play literally and figuratively focuses on *El Hombre* who is seen in the middle of the stage on his deathbed. The bed itself, of a "monumental" size, is placed on top of a platform and can be reached by a stairway on either side of the platform. The focus on the bed is accentuated by the semicircle of white columns against a black background. The Man himself does not act or speak except to agonize from time to time at the hour of his death. Rather, the play's eight scenes present the Man's friends and family as they reveal their pedantry and hypocrisy while discussing the life of this great man whom they are incapable of understanding.

The central question of this *esbozo* appears in the first scene in the words of *el Amigo Político* who says: "Y luego, hay que saber lo que significa la gloria de un hombre grande. En momentos como éste, se entiende" (13). As the three friends, the Poet, the Philosopher, and the Politician, discuss this question, they reveal their own jealousy and incapability of transcendence to immortality. Ironically, their conversation reveals to the spectator/reader a glimpse of the Man's true greatness juxtaposed to the corresponding "smallness" of these three characters.

The following five scenes create a similar effect. The Man's Wife and Son (Stepson of the Wife), who have a sexual relationship, conspire to poison him and thus to inherit his wealth; the Son and the Nurse have a similar relationship, although the Nurse alone shows some compassion for her moribund patient. Subsequent scenes involving the Nurse and the Servant, the Priest, and once again, the

Son and Woman, serve to make obvious the same dichotomy between the "smallness" of these common people and the "greatness" of the Man who has an unquenched thirst for immortality. To focus further on this dichotomy, the sounds of a dance in another part of the house serve as a backdrop to the hypocritical conversatiions that take place as the Man lies dying. Various other sounds communicate the actual death, including the Woman's convulsive laughter, bells, the Priest's monotonous voice and others, when they achieve a cacophonous stage of chaos, followed by a sudden, abrupt silence.

The following two scenes correspond to the profundity of the theme and the triviality of the characters, again illuminating the pre-established dichotomy in the Man's life. Immediately following the death, three shadows—Black, Red and Blue—fight for the Man's soul, the Black representing the spiritual in the form of religion as well as superstition, and ignorance; the Red, the carnal and materialistic; while the Blue, which wins in the end, is the shadow of the Man's own work and *is* his immortality. The Blue Shadow expresses what the spectator will already have perceived as the work's basic premise: "Por vuestra culpa es la vida del Hombre una horrible tortura. Y llegáis hasta su lecho en esta hora para gozaros en vuestra obra. Pero no es la vuestra la que cuenta. Es la obra del Hombre.... ¡La suya! Su propia creación. En la que puso tanto de sí mismo que ya no podía morir. Vivirá este hombre en la memoria de la Humanidad para siempre. Hasta ese tiempo absoluto que llamáis eternidad" (p. 39). The Blue Shadow's euphoria is accompanied by bells and a blue light focusing on the Man, who responds by sitting up with an expression of joy on his face. The moment's enchantment is broken by a return to the temporal level as the Man is once more seen as before under a yellow light and the Woman, Son, and Nurse continue their hypocrisy of earlier scenes, thus ending the play on a critical note in its view of contemporary society and the manner in which that society responds to artistic creativity.

The dramatic elements which give life to this play are evident throughout René Marqués' playwriting career. The technique for which he is perhaps most remembered is the infusing of symbolic meaning into different colored lights with which he often isolates and accentuates his characters' unique characteristics. In this play, the author spells out the color symbolism through the appearance of the three shadows. In later plays, especially *Los soles truncos*, his communication of meaning is much more subtle.

At about the same time, Marqués wrote another play, entitled _Palm Sunday_. He wrote the play in 1949 in English while studying drama at Columbia University in New York City. This early play presents most clearly how the political crisis which preoccupies the author affects the personal life of the Puerto Rican. The play concerns the events just prior to the "Ponce Massacre" which occurred on Palm Sunday, March 21, 1937, and ends with the disastrous event itself. In that historic event, a group of Nationalist Cadets, having received permission from Ponce's mayor, staged a march in support of Nationalist leader Pedro Albizu Campos. At the last minute, Governor Blanton Winship ordered the mayor to withdraw the permission. When the Cadets continued their parade, they were surrounded by police, some unknown person opened fire, and when the shooting ended twenty-one people were dead—some of them, uninvolved bystanders.

Marqués' dramatization of the event is the first literary incursion into that disaster in Puerto Rico and a bold one if we consider the short time span between the historic event and the writing of the play. The play, however, while produced once (1956 in the Tapia Theatre by _Teatro Nuestro_) has not been published. This work is very important in its relationship to the author's later works inasmuch as it foreshadows the central crisis of his major plays as well as their characters and dramatic relationships.

The play takes place in the Drawing Room of Governor John Winfield and the principal characters are the Governor, his Puerto Rican wife, Mercedes, and their son, Alberto. The conflict develops on two planes: on a political level, it results from the mayor's having granted the Cadets permission to parade. The Nationalist element is one the Governor cannot tolerate since it implies the undermining of United States control, and by extension, his own power over Puerto Rico. On the personal level, we learn that the Governor's son sympathizes with the Nationalists on the basis of his being Puerto Rican, and through the play's development, makes this known to his father as both reject each other's ideals. In the end, Alberto witnesses, from the balcony, the death of the flag bearer, his friend. He goes and carries the flag himself, is shot and is killed. Mercedes, throughout, is torn between her love for her husband and for her son—two sides diametrically opposed because of the political conflict. Mercedes' role has the effect of revealing the prejudices her husband in fact feels towards Puerto Ricans in general. As in Marqués' other plays, the inner personal conflict here is closely related to the political one, and the Governor, it seems, was once a liberal whose ideals of freedom became stagnant when he had to choose between standing up for those beliefs or solidifying his own individual power. The two choices are mutually exclusive and the Governor chooses the latter.)

It is quite easy to see parallels between these three characters and those of the well-known plays, *Un niño azul para esa sombra* and *La muerte no entrará en palacio*. Alberto, in his inner conflict, is a vivid reminder of Michelín, the child protagonist of *Un niño azul*, as well as of Casandra, the Governor's daughter, in *La muerte. . .* (Governor John Winship himself embodies the same pattern of lost ideals as does the Governor in *La muerte no entrará en palacio.* At the same time, his former ideals are the same as those of Michel in *Un niño azul para esa sombra*. Nowhere does this analogy stand out more than in Alberto's words to his father near the end of Act I:

> I remember when I was a little kid. . . . You knew so many things . . .
> you understood everything so well. Remember the day I caught the
> "bien te veo"? I wanted to put it in a cage. I thought it would like the
> cage . . . it was a beautiful cage—and big. But you said, "Let's see if he
> likes it. Put him in the cage, but leave the door open. Give him a chance
> to choose." I did. The bird flew away. I cried, but you said, "Don't be
> sorry. You did the right thing. All creatures choose freedom when they
> are given a choice." That was a long time ago. . . . (ms. copy 13-14)

This caged bird anticipates one in *Un niño azul* which Michelín frees in the play's opening scene. And, of course, the whole "jailed" image is the basis of the expression of Michel's failure and of Michelín's dilemma.

Mercedes of *Palm Sunday* anticipates several of Marqués' women, but especially the wife of Don José in *La muerte* and Mercedes, mother of Michelín, in *Un niño azul*. The former is totally loyal to her Puerto Rican identity while the latter has given in to the materialistic ideals which Marqués associated negatively with the United States' influence in Puerto Rico. The Mercedes of *Palm Sunday* has the potential to be either one of the two later characters, but since in the early play she never is given the chance to choose, she remains undeveloped on that level. Through its historic theme, this early play written in English and as a class assignment, reveals the same inner conflict which was created more poetically in Michelín and Casandra. At the same time, it emphasizes the cultural and ideological conflicts between the Puerto Rican and the North American at the base of nearly all of Marqués' subsequent works.

More than any of the other early plays, *El sol y los MacDonald,* written and premiered in 1950 and published in 1957, anticipates the theatrically rich and self-disciplined author of the later plays. In the plays written before this one, form and content seem to be off balance—form outweighing content in *El hombre y sus sueños* and content weighing more heavily than form in *Palm Sunday.* In *El sol y los MacDonald,* there is a much greater equilibrium between the two. The three-act play concerns the last generation of a proud and in-bred plantation family from the United States South. The original family pride which would admit neither foreigners nor people of other races—especially Blacks—into the blood-line is responsible for the incestuous feelings between mother and son in the play's two representative generations. These tendencies become a curse which causes the demise of the family name. The themes of egotism, discrimination, incest and isolation take second place to the inexorable passage of time which motivates the eventual decadence in which the play's characters live. The mask motif underlies the stylistic presentation as well as the ultimate message and is revealed through the futile and meaningless recourses of these characters to give the appearance of living in the "real" world. They have, in fact, withdrawn into an infernal world of their own making.

The play presents two generations of the MacDonald family: 1) Gustavo, the oldest, his two sisters Elisa and Teodora, and the latter's husband, Enrique García; and 2) Ramiro García, the son of Teodora and Enrique. The three-act structure depends on the developing parallels between Gustavo and his nephew Ramiro which in turn serve as catalyst to all the major conflicts in the work. Each act begins with the projected thoughts of either Gustavo or Ramiro, and then proceeds to affirm those thoughts in actions. The play's first opening scenes consist of Gustavo's thoughts as he plays the role of marginal observer. His audible thinking introduces the spectator to each of the characters, the principal themes, and insinuates the underlying conflict. The act ends when the young Ramiro, out of jealousy, shoots his Aunt Elisa's suitor in an open attempt to kill him.

Act Two takes place ten years later and opens with a similar scene in which Ramiro's thoughts continue to develop the parallels between him and his uncle. A key event in this act which serves to unify the play is a scene in which Ramiro and his mother display an incestuous attraction for each other. However, they continually try to resist the expression of those strong feelings. Ramiro, left alone, ponders the reasons for the incest and in a dream-like presentation is witness to three flashback scenes which reveal similar tendencies in the family's preceding generations, starting with hatred of foreigners and Blacks and resulting in in-breeding and finally the incestuous—though always unfulfilled—attractions between mother and son. The act's final encounter, between Ramiro and Gustavo, affirms the parallels, now well-established, but suggests rather implicitly that Ramiro still has two possible avenues of action—to leave the family home and free himself from the bonds that hold all the others, or to stay and continue to live under the shadow of the "curse."

The third act occurs two years later and begins, as did the first, with Gustavo's thoughts while he observes the rest of the family. Quite clearly, during the twelve year period, nothing has changed. In this final act, however, Ramiro sees the family in an objective way and serves as their conscience. One by one, he strips his family of their masks and finally accuses them of being motivated not by pride but rather by fear. He then is able to overcome the MacDonald side of his nature and to escape "to life," as he says. The others all return to the security of their "masks" behind which they escape from life outside of the family circle, symbolized in Teodora's knitting, Enrique's newspaper, and Gustavo's thoughts.

Technically, Marqués resorts to the standard concept of chronological time to create within the family house a stagnant and isolated world which protects the family from outside reality at the same time as it masks the fear which is the true motivation for their narcissism. The inner thoughts of Gustavo and Ramiro which introduce their respective acts have as background blue light and eerie music, while other characters often simultaneously carry out the actions that the thoughts describe. Each act, then, to a degree, affirms what the inner thoughts suggest. A similar created subjectivity presents the retrospective scenes of Act Two, played out behind transparent gauze curtains with blue light and the rhythmic sound of horses' hooves. These scenes, then, do not merely reveal past events, but rather seem to emanate from the characters'—or perhaps even the house's—inner being. In his later plays, René Marqués perfected much of what carries this play forward dramatically. Most possibly, the best later-developed theatrical devices are the embodiment of time as a villainous accomplice in the passage of life and the creation of a family space (i.e., the house) which imprisons and isolates while it also protects. In some cases, this family space even serves as a mask to hide the true inner feelings of its inhabitants, an effect most evident in the author's highly lauded work, *Los soles truncos*.

Los condenados, an early play of René Marqués once thought lost or destroyed, is dated June, 1951, and was produced for the first time in 1982 during the Ateneo Puertorriqueño's René Marqués Festival. The work is a technically advanced drama reminiscent in many ways of several of the later plays, paticularly of the confined world of *Los soles truncos* and of many of Marqués' characters who try to mold their own world but fail to accept the reality that surrounds them.

The list of characters consists of five men and one woman, the latter serving as catalyst in the play's dramatic development. Aside from the *Llanero* who is not a major character, the others are surrounded by an aura of religious fanaticism in which each tries to create or in some way fulfill his or her own individual dreams. Miguel, the religious fanatic, in his egotism is trying to avoid seeing God, while his nephew, Rodrigo, attempts just the opposite. José, an alcoholic and would-be author, dreams of the novel he will never write, while the deformed Pedro's dream is to create a balance between Miguel's fanaticism and reality. María dreams of the child of love which she believes she will bear as God has mandated. These "dreams," however, prove to be handicaps inasmuch as they prevent the characters from confronting the reality of the world from which they are trying to escape. Their insistence on holding onto their dreams condemns them to a frustrating, non-productive life. As the play develops, the characters' efforts to sustain their own individual dreams end in death or moral destruction for all but the woman, María, and the youngest of the men, Rodrigo. But even their survival is only a restrained suggestion of hope since it is based on the continuance of their own excapist dreams.

Throughout the play, the tension between escapism and reality is constant. Technically, the desert setting with its scarcity of water reflects the sterility of the world presented on stage. The entrance of the woman into the masculine world coincides with a storm's outbreak on the outside. As the water begins to leak into the room, the sound of the dripping serves as an ever-present reminder of the outside reality. The storm's outbreak symbolizes that of the torment on the inside, too, with the deaths first of José, then of Miguel, and ending with that of Pedro.

In this play, as in many of Marqués dramatic works, the entire action develops within the living quarters which protect its inhabitants from the threatening world outside. The characters, who are not a blood family, are related spiritually, and together have created a world of religious fanaticism where they can mutually support one another's reasons for being there. They condemn themselves, then, to this life which is totally sterile and non-productive making the deaths at the end no more than an extension of their life. These same concepts—again, the protective living quarters, the self-created, escapist world, and self-condemnation or implicity of guilt—will be the foundation stones of all of the later plays.

The topics of the following chapters loosely unite the plays subsequent to those already discussed in ways that serve to point out the major elements of the body of René Marqués' theatrical creations. The topics themselves are directly related to his use of space and time as dynamic forces on the stage, and the fact that a given work falls into one category or another, does not exclude it from having a relationship to others. The categories into which particular plays are grouped, however, do indicate the dynamic forces at the heart of those plays.

Chapter III

Coetaneity and Contiguity

René Marqués' two widely acclaimed plays, *Los soles truncos* (1958) and *Un niño azul para esa sombra* (1958), both depend on the integration of space and time in such a way that past, present, and future, as well as their respective corresponding spaces coexist in the virtual worlds created on stage. In each of these works, multiple signs draw the spectator/reader's attention toward the spatial and temporal configurations whose coetaneous and contiguous nature brings to life the underlying crises at the center of each play's development.

In an article entitled "The Spatial Dimension of Theatre," Stanley Vincent Longman affirms that "theatre involves the presence of at least three realms: stage, house, and off-stage; it develops its spatial dimensions by characterizing, vivifying, and multiplying the three realms" (46). Longman would simultaneously take into consideration a play's temporal dimension since the double reliance on time and space, according to him, "is one of the most difficult elements of theatre art" (59). Marqués, in *Los soles truncos*, dynamically creates within the work three spatial dimensions. Signs directed toward the audience integrate the various spaces while communicating the disastrous effects of time within the play's realms, and by extension, within that of the spectators.

Los soles truncos, based on Marqués short story, "Purificación en la Calle del Cristo," dramatizes the story of the three Burkhart sisters, of German and Spanish descent, whose parents had been wealthy landowners during the period of Spanish colonialism in Puerto Rico and after Spain's ceding of the island to the United States. We encounter two of the sisters, Inés and Emilia, now elderly spinsters, living in the family house in Old San Juan, at the moment of the third sister, Hortensia's, death. Throughout the play, we find the sisters embroiled not only in an external conflict with the materialistic worlds which surround their family house, but also in an internal conflict among and within themselves, revealed through the appearance of the dead sister. The obvious physical and spiritual decadence in which the three have lived out their own drama reveals them to be as much victims of their own inability to confront the changing outside reality, as they are victims of the socio-political conditions existing in Puerto Rico. The world on the outside constantly threatens to bring an end to the one which they have created within, so that at the end of the play, they make the decision to destroy the house and themselves by fire as an ironic solution to giving meaning to their inevitable destruction.)

The play's development depends on the creation of four distinct spaces—two on stage, and two offstage—each of which also has a corresponding temporal dimension. The on-stage realms are the anachronistic present reality in which the sisters live—distinct from the "outside" present—and the anachronistic appearances of the recently-deceased sister—an illusory past which evokes the worlds of Strasbourg, Germany and of the Tao Alta plantation in Puerto Rico, while at the same time they bring to the surface secrets within each of the sisters which have been the real motives for their withdrawal from life. The first offstage realm is the world immediately beyond the house, or the "outside" present, but is still within the confines of the play. The space which the audience occupies becomes a fourth realm, completing the dramatic experience. According to Longman, "the 'house' or audience's space is the most crucial realm of theatrical experience. It is the point of contrast between the contrivances of the actors and the stage, on the one hand, and the reality of human experience on the other" (47). Through the integration of the spatial and temporal dimensions within the play itself, Marqués penetrates the space of the public, creating for the spectators an emotional experience akin to that of the characters themselves.

(Penetration becomes a dramatic technique throughout the course of the play that serves not only to move the action forward but also to depict the constant threat of violation to the sisters' world. A repeated pattern of domination of one or more of the realms over another heightens the tension and creates the rhythm governing the play's movement. The stage setting fuses and at the same time separates the play's several realms, further enhancing lines of tension between play and audience. The truncated windows, the house itself, as well as props, strategically used, signify for the spectators and the characters the irrevocable passage of time despite all efforts to combat its destructive force.

The most dramatic and noticeable incursion of one space/time configuration into another comes near the end of Act II. Tamara Holzapfel says of this scene: "A state of unrelieved anguish, created by the passing of time, is the dominant mood of the play and is especially heightened in the final scene as the present threatens to break into the house in the form of the violent knocking at the door" ("The Theatre of René Marqués: In Search of Identity and Form" 155). We find the action in the illusory realm of the spinsters' evoked past. In this scene all three are present as they vividly envision the funeral march upon their father's death. At this point, we actually witness a fusing of all four realms as the immediate outside world attempts to penetrate the inner world of the house. Inés remembers desperate knocks on the heavy door of the hacienda at Toa Alta as they received news of their father's death. At the same instant in the play, we hear knocks on the door of the house of Cristo Street. Throughout the remainder of this scene, the rhythmic cadence of the funeral march replaces the blows on the door as the dream-like realm of the past dominates the action. At the end, however, the outside world abruptly destroys the illusion. The stage directions guide our perception of this penetration as Inés finishes speaking:

> (Al extinguirse la voz, se oye un golpetear estruendoso sobre el portalón de ausubo, en el zaguán. Cesa simultáneamente la marcha fúnebre, se apaga la luz y surge de súbito, la iluminación normal que viene del exterior, fondo. . . . Sigue oyéndose el golpear con puños y palmas en el portalón de ausubo. . . .) (In *Teatro*, Tomo I, 54)

The knocks on the door from the exterior present bring the play suddenly back from the space of the past into the more immediate world. Words such as *estruendoso, simultáneamente,* and *de súbito,* as well as Emilia's subsequent reaction of fear to the blows on the door, communicate the violent nature of this interruption. Penetrations throughout the play culminate in this *one* which forces immediate action on the part of Emilia and Inés.

The house, various props, sound, light, and color, serve double purposes as they represent the pssage of time and also unite for brief moments two or more of the spatial/temporal realms. The house serves first a very practical purpose as the dwelling place of the play's antagonists. In this sense, because of the fact that it divides the inner present world from the outside world, it signifies the presence of that larger, immediate exterior realm. The absence of any direct physical connection on stage with the other side maintains an ever-present tension between those two spaces. Secondly, seen in its stage of deterioration and shadow, it also serves as a visual representation to the audience of the state of the sisters' present world. Angelina Morfi notes this aspect of the play in her *Historia crítica de un siglo de teatro puertorriqueño:* "Aparecen deslustrados, desvaídos, desteñidos, deteriorados, adjetivos y participios con el prefijo des, con que René Marqués logra marcar con fuerza el paso del tiempo" (498). The world represented in the houses's deterioration and in its contents is the past history of its occupants filtered through their present situation, further maintaining tension between these two realms.

Various props also provide a point of contact between the two interior spaces. One of the more obvious is the candelabra which in Act I is either lit or extinguished before each of Hortensia's two appearances. Inés' extinguishing of the candle mysteriously signals Hortensia's first entrance and the transference of action to the level of the evoked past. The stage directions describe the event:

> (. . . va a la consola y apaga la bujía. Al hacerlo se oye un sonido musical extraño, como la cuerda de un instrumento que se rompe. Simultáneamente languidece la luz mañanera del exterior que se cuela por los soles truncos y la persiana. . . .) (19)

Extinguishing the candle sets off a chain reaction which breaks the bounds of logic and gives the illusion of suspending the passage of time as the scene now occupies the somewhat different space of the past.

In addition, sounds coming from offstage serve to enhance our perception of the tension between the various realms, thus forcing us as spectators to intensify our attention focused on the element of time. Voices fulfill an important dramatic and auditory function. At the beginning of both acts, the voice of the Street Vendor penetrates the house from the outside world as his words coming to the audience through the on-stage present take on an ironic meaning. The dialog of the play's opening scene is one of voices shifting back and forth between the physical levels of the stage as well as the spatial realms of the play. Inés enters calling for Emilia. We hear Emilia's response from the upstairs rooms. By the time Emilia enters, Inés has left. This time Emilia's words, to no one in particular, are followed by Inés' voice coming now from Hortensia's room on the lower level. Emilia, startled by the voice, then calls to Inés but receives no answer. Her

speech and actions, however, lead the audience to "listen" to the Street
Vendor's words:

> EMILIA—Inés. (Al no recibir contestación, siempre indecisa, baja otro
> escalón.) ¿Duermes, Hortensia? (Pausa. Retrocede, subiendo de
> espaldas, el escalón que acaba de bajar.) ¿Sigues dormida, Hortensia?
> (Escucha atentamente. Al no percibir sonido alguno, su rostro se
> tranquiliza, finalmente sonríe y, volviéndose, sube otra vez de prisa, y
> sale.) (11)

Emilia's quiet manner plus her indecisiveness on the stairway, followed by her attentive listening and the complete silence on stage
force the spectator to hear the words of the Street Vendor who then
passes by on the outside selling his seductive wares:

> VOZ DEL PREGONERO—¡Malrayo, polvo de amor, besitos de coco,
> pruébalos, doña! ¡Malraaayo, polvo de amor, besitos de coco para
> endulzarse el alma, cómprelos, doña! ¡Malraaayo, polvo de amor,
> besitos bonitos de cocooo. . . ! (12)

As the outside world once again penetrates the sisters' inner sanctum,
we perceive the ironic nature of his words since it is apparent that
these ladies have no means by which to purchase his delicious wares.
Simultaneously, this intrusion makes most obvious the existence of
two distinct and incompatible worlds, one inside the house, the other
outside.

Music also enhances our perception of the various spatial/
temporal realms of the play. On the level of the present within the
house, we hear Emilia's humming. As various scenes move toward or
into the dream-like sequences, however, the music comes from an
offstage orchestra or a piano, neither seen nor acknowledged in any
way by the play's characters. The music is directly intended for the
audience's perception and interpretation within the respective scenes.
This music corresponds to the action in much the same way to which
we are accustomed in the cinema. The music of Richard Wagner's Die
Walküre music is planned to add an extra dimension to the work. In
Act I, during her first appearance, Hortensia opens the way for this
association. Inés has compared her sister to their blond father:

> INES—Es hermoso como un dios nórdico.
> HORTENSIA—(Riendo) Lo cual me convierte a mí en Walkiria. Por lo
> menos. (21)

The closing scene of the play calls to mind the final scene of Wagner's opera in which Brunhilde lies asleep surrounded by red flames. In Marqués' play, the scenic directions again set the picture: "El vuelo del traje y el velo de encajes caen flotantes alrededor del ataúd casi ocultándolo" (61). Here, Hortensia lies as if on a funeral pyre rather than in a beggar's casket. As the light of the fire set by Inés and Emilia begins to appear, the volume of the music increases correspondingly, and Hortensia seems very much like Wagner's Brunhilde. These stage directions bring the play to a majestic end: "La música de Wagner sube apoteótica. La sala toda es un infierno purificador" (66). The sisters' present reality wins out over the immediate outside world and their death is neither macabre nor grotesque, but rather, ironically heroic.

Light and color are intricately linked to each of the spatial/ temporal realms. In Act I, the elements of light and color are the very first to be set in the stage directions: "Sobre cada una de las puertas hay un semicírculo de cristales en tres colores alternadoes: rojo, azul, amarillo.... La luz exterior sólo entra a través de los soles truncos" (7). Sam Smiley, in *Playwriting: A Structure of Action,* says that one of the functions of light in a play is that it "commands attention" (195). Commanding attention is its most important function here since the light from the outside gives shape to the interior of the house and thus to the audience's perception of the sisters' inner world. Multiple interpretations of the symbolic nature of this light exist. Loreina Santos Silva says: "Nos situamos ante una luz que no se realiza porque en vano trata de penetrar 'soles truncos' en el aspecto físico y espiritual" ("Reflexiones sobre *Los soles truncos* 63). Howard Fraser suggests that "the treatment of light corresponds to the erosion of lucidity in the sisters' minds" ("Theatricality" 6). Both of these interpretations seem to be supported by the plays dialogue and action. There is certainly no doubt that the sun, as a symbol of time, is the enemy. Emilia makes this association at the play's opening as she accuses the sun as if it were an adversary: "El sol no me deja peinar.... Es el sol, te digo. Yo no tengo la culpa. Es el sol" (10). Importantly, it is the sun that is the enemy—not the light *per se*—for the sun represents the passage of time, and therefore further implicates the temporal element in the decadence visualized in the play.

Dramatically, each of the three colors is linked to a spatial/ temporal realm. The yellow becomes associated with the immediate outside world, and the sun's light. Except for the dream-like

sequences in which Hortensia appears and all natural light in extinguished, it is constantly present as a reminder of that exterior world
and of the threat that the other space and time pose to the sisters'
interior world. At the beginning of Act II, the scene is unchanged
except for this light: "La luz exterior que entra por los cristales del
fondo es más intensa a esta hora que en el acto anterior" (40). At this
point the yellow light functions in two ways: one, it indicates the
passage of time in the play's action from morning to afternoon; and
two, it emphasizes the growing force of the outside world as antago-
nist.

The color blue is linked to the illusory past through Hortensia's
three stage appearances. In each of these scenes, the blue light
accompanies Hortensia, and at the end of the play illuminates her
deathbed. As the blue light dominates in each of these scenes, the
normal light is extinguished, thus anticipating Hortensia's entrances
as well as indicating that normal time has ceased flowing while the
past realm controls the scene.

Red dominates the play's final scene as the flames spread
throughout the house. The color intensifies as the volume of the music
increases, creating a cinematographic effect. The red reflections
appear first in one place and then another: "Cuando Inés va por la
mitad de la escalera, se puede observar que, a sus espaldas, provi-
niendo de las habitaciones superiores, surgen reflejos rojizos." Then,
"Del vestíbulo empiezan a surgir reflejos rojizos" (624); and, "De la
habitación de la derecha que acaba de abandonar INES empiezan a
surgir relfejos rojizos" (65). Finally, as the flames gain even greater
intensity: "Al fondo, en el exterior de la casa empiezan a surgir reflejos
anaranjados, cuya intensidad aumenta con rapidez hasta iluminar
fantásticamente los soles truncos de las tres puertas cerrades" (65).
The red appears a little at a time as if a camera were photographing the
scene until the red shades overpower the blue light and the exterior
light is extinguished. As the sisters break all ties with the outside, their
present realm dominates. The tense bonds with the outside world are
severed while the past is at the same time paid for and immortalized.
That final moment lives forever in the public realm since we do not
witness the death of the sisters but rather their decision carried into
action.

The final scenes of Los soles truncos, beginning with the blows
on the door to the grandiose finale, integrate the play's three spatial/
temporal realms. Through lines of tension which the recurrent pattern

of penetration and the dramatic signals have created, the integrated space/time configurations reach into the world of the audience. The play's exterior present, the present world inside the house, and the illusory past evoked within the house in combination with the auditory and visual signs, invite the theatre public's vicarious participation in the sisters' final victory over indecisiveness and inaction. As the Burkharts sever the ties, and thus the threat, with the outside realm, they definitively bring an end to that incompatible world's penetration into their own.

René Marqués play, *Un niño azul para esa sombra,* written in 1958, won the "Eugenio Fernández García" theatre prize that same year in the Ateneo Puertorriqueño's Christmas Festival. This play, produced two years later, during the Third Theatre Festival sponsored by the Institute of Puerto Rican Culture, is, according to Frank Dauster, "probably Marqués' best play," and, "one of the best in Latin America" ("New Plays of René Marqués" 452). Like *Los soles truncos,* it is thematically based on previously-written short stories: in this case, "La sala" (1956) "El niño en el árbol" (1958) and, perhaps, "El juramento" (1955) (*En una ciudad llamada San Juan*). In this work, Marqués experiments not only with the chronological presentation of the story, but also with the play's foreward movement. Structurally, the present surrounds and contains the past until the suicidal death of the child protagonist in the final moments. At that point, the child's past affirms his identity.

The play tells the story of the child Michelín, caught between the liberationist ideals of his father and the materialistic, Northamericanized world of his mother. Although the play's various elements can be dichotomized between the two sides, and Michelín undoubtedly belongs on the freedom side, his position is really much more complex than would appear on the surface. The liberty for which Michelín struggles is that of the individual's right to his own unique identity. This child, is prevented from exercising that right because of the "shadows" that prevail in his life. His mother, Mercedes, controls his physical world, and he lives in the material luxury that has resulted from the choices his mother has made in her life. His emotional, inner world, however, depends on a self-created, false relationship with a non-existent father. This illusory relationship was originally encouraged by his father's adopted sister, Cecilia, but later developed as an integral part of Michelín's own imagined world. Both sets of values— the mother's and the father's—so dominate Michelín's life that he is constantly torn between them with no opportunity to develop any meaningful values that are truly his own. In the end, the only freedom which Michelín can exercize is that of choosing to create the circumstances of his own death.

Acts I and III take place on Michelín's tenth birthday as the tension of waiting for the play's *denouement* parallels that of waiting for the arrival of the birthday party guests. The first act introduces Michelín's solitary world, based on dreams and illusions, in which his own anguish becomes related to his mother's poisoning of a large *quenepo* tree which once shaded the terrace and had been for the child a father-figure and make-believe protector. The retrospective second act takes place two years prior to both Acts I and III. This portion of the play, portrayed as part of Michelín's dream, establishes the tension between the child's past and his imminent future, thus creating his present moment—a present which contains both past and future. In Act II we witness not only the dissolution of the parents' marriage and the total destruction of his father's future, but the beginning of the child's own self-destruction as well. Act III brings the child back to reality and to the moments preceding the party. In this act, he is confronted with the reality of his father's death and the falseness of the dream world in which he attempts to survive. This knowledge forces him to act, and suicide becomes a logical and heroic choice.

Through a series of interrelated signals transmitted to the audience, the play creates the impression of temporal coetaneity which signifies a life and death crisis for the child protagonist. Michelín, who finds himself trapped between the heroic ideals of his father and the worldly values of his mother, embodies a two-dimensional crisis: that of the anguished individual within the realm of humanity; and that of the island of Puerto Rico under the shadow of a large and powerful nation. Time does not merely "stand still." Rather like the child, it appears to be trapped in a vacuum. In the temporal approach which Marqués takes in this work, the second act is of prime importance. Because the action occurs as part of the child's dream, no time actually passes in the play's story. In addition, although hours and minutes obviously do pass in the playing time of the drama, the audience is swept up by the illusion that time has stopped for a short while. Because of the nature of the second act, past, present and future coexist in a world of circular, rather than forward, movement. This combination of circular movement and temporal coetaneity guides us to an understanding of the present, real anguish which Michelín suffers, and of the symbolic meaning behind his death.

Circularity is apparent in the lineal structure of the work, the stage setting, and the imagery. In the first and third acts, the birthday party motif calls attention to the play's structural ellipsis. The work opens and closes on the protagonist's tenth birthday. Michelín has invited a friend, Andrés, to come earlier than his other party guests, all of whom, except Andrés, have been invited by Mercedes. Andrés' presence serves to reinforce the play's temporal circularity:

> ANDRES—Oye, ¿a qué hora empieza la fiesta?
> MICHELIN—A la tarde.
> ANDRES—¿Y por qué me hiciste venir tan temprano? (80)

From this moment on we wait, with Andrés, for the celebration to begin. In Act II, the image of the birthday is implicitly present. As Michel, the child's father, re-experiences his eight-year imprisonment for revolutionary activities, the author's stage directions subtly reintroduce the birthday image:

> (. . . Se oye un llanto de un niño de un año de edad. No es el llanto inconsciente y chillón de un bebé, sino el llanto de una criatura que empieza a descubrir con horror la vida. Michel se vuelve bruscamente hacia el fondo. El llanto arrecia),

and he shouts, "¡Michelín!" (118). Although the cries are not those of a newborn infant, the fact that they *are* associated with the child protagonist as a baby brings to mind for the audience the idea of his birth, and by extension, the party which has yet to take place from Act I. Act III finalizes this image in the last scene as the offstage guests ironically sing "Happy Birthday," in English, to Michelín, who hangs dead on the trellis of the terrace. His birthday anniversary and his birth itself coexist with the moment of his death, therefore making the play's physical structure also a temporal one in which beginning and end, or past and present, meet.

The stage setting creates the illusion of entrapment and is a physical representation of Michelín's own feeling of imprisonment. Acts I and III take place on the terrace, while Act II develops in the living room of the luxurious mansion. In both spaces, there are several supposed exits which, in fact, do not connect directly to the world outside. In the terrace scenes, a glass door opens upon the terrace from the living room. The terrace itself is surrounded by a railing which has one opening into the yard and another open space where the *quenepo* once stood, and where the trellis on which Michelín dies now stands. The author describes this latter opening as follows: "En el centro mismo, fondo de la terraza, la baranda está partida dejando un espacio que hubiera podido ser salida del jardín" (71). This description tells us, as the stage setting would show us, that this space is not an exit even though it might have been so once. Ironically, it does serve as a way out for Michelín at the play's end when he dies there.

The living room of Act II has several dimensions of height and depth, as well as several exits from the room such as the stairway on which we see Michelín as he witnesses the confrontation between his parents, and the vestibule which connects to a hall, and we only assume, finally out of the house. At the very back of this area there hangs a large portrait of Mercedes, seemingly guarding any exits from the house and giving even more depth to the scene. The glass door at stage left is the one that opens onto the terrace, which as we know from the previous act, is also enclosed, thus intensifying the illusion of there being no exit.

In this Marqués play, the accumulating impressions and images of entrapment and death work harmoniously with the structure and the *mise-en-scene* to communicate to the audience Michelín's feeling of anguish and utter helplessness and to support further the creation of the "no exit" concept. Act I integrates many of these images directly into the dramatic presentation, while in Act II, they appear expressionistically in the scene depicting Michel's suffering, as well as in the dialogue between the parents. By the end of the third and final act, Michelín's suicidal death is the logical extension of these accumulated impressions.

The opening scene introduces the idea of imprisonment as well as of death. Michelín enters carrying a caged canary across the terrace into the garden where we assume he frees the little bird. Immediately following this action, and as the invited guest calls for his host from offstage, Cecilia, also offstage, sings a song about a dead child. This song dramatically associates Michelín with death as it subsequently becomes part of an offstage dialogue between the child protagonist and Cecilia:

MICHELIN—(Su voz fuera de escena) ¡Cecilia! ¡Cállate!

CECILIA—(Su voz más lejana en el interior)
  El niñito muerto
  Ya va para el cielo,
  Los ángeles cantan
  en el cementerio.
MICHELIN—(Su voz fuera de escena, histérica ahora) ¡Cállate!
¡Cállate! No quiero oír esa canción. ¡Cállate! (77)

If the spectator does not, as a normal reaction, associate the song with the child, Michelín's strong, hysterical reaction forces such an association to take place. This act further creates a parallel between the child and death in the dream-like sequence depicting Mercedes' assassination of the *quenepo,* and again in the final dream sequence as the boy's father, closing the child's eyes by placing his hand over them, asks a blessing on his son.

In Act II, both parents bequeath an inheritance of imprisonment to their son. On a darkened stage from which we hear only his voice, the father, Michel, expresses the anguish of his eight-year confinement:

No es fácil convertir en sonido los pensamientos propios cuando hay tantos años de silencio—o de casi silencio—envolviéndolo todo: la luz matinal y la medianoche, la soledad, el cuerpo, la ventana y la puerta; los pasos, las manos. . . . ¡Todo en fin! ¡Calado hasta los huesos de silencio! Las palabras circulando en el alma sin salida; ¡prisioneras del tiempo, sin espacio! (120)

These words express not only the physical confinement which reduced Michel's world to a window, a door and his own footsteps as he paced back and forth, but also the silencing of his thoughts and ideas, for which there is no outlet. In this same act, Mercedes reveals that she, too, feels imprisoned: "Y las puertas cerradas. Como si las del presidio al cerrarse diera la señal a todas las puertas del mundo: 'Ciérrense, puertas, ciérrense bien' " (136). She adds in the same conversation: "sólo quiero que sepas que también yo supe del horror de sentirme prisionera" (137). Ironically, Mercedes' "prison" is that fear of being excluded from the world to which she aspires so that she is, in a sense, trapped outside rather than inside. The legacy, then, that the child Michelín inherits from both father and mother is one of stagnation, and of the frustration of unrealized dreams.

Evidence of death and destruction prevails throughout the play, providing perhaps the only apparent progression in the work.

The assassination of the tree in Act I and the violent acts against the tin Statue of Liberty in Act II culminate in Michelín's suicide in the final act. The depiction of those events in the order in which they are presented, while out of chronological sequence, makes the sacrificial suicide of Michelín the logical ending for the play. In the acting out of the tree's assassination, Michelín feels the pain of death as his tree—friend dies. According to the stage directions: "MICHELIN, quien observa la escena de espaldas a nosotros, se va encorvando, replegándose en sí mismo, como si sintiera los efectos del veneno, hasta que cae de rodillas mordiéndose los puños" (89). This empathy and self-induced suffering reveal to the audience, in the play's early stages, the boy's psychological state.

In Act II, we see the motivating factors behind the child's violent tendencies and ultimate self-destruction. This act culminates in Michelín's violent act of aggression against a replica of the Statue of Liberty which stands near his house. (Such a statue does in fact stand on the Avenida Ashford in the Condado district of San Juan and was indeed defaced by vandals at one time.) His defacing of the statue, which for him represents both his mother as the destroyer of his own personal world, and the United States as the destroyer of his father's ideals, makes clear his own preoccupations as well as his violent tendencies.

In Act III, although we do not see Michelín ingest the poison, all of these past impressions of death point towards that logical end. Each successive destructive act involves Michelín more than the previous one. Although he apparently feels pain as he witnesses the tree's death, he is merely an observer of the ceremony. His mother commits the act. He himself carries out the attack in the second act, but directs it toward someone else. In Act III, as the circle closes in on the child and he cannot escape, he aims his destructiveness at himself.

We further sense the frustration of movement as we detect strong parallels between the young boy of Acts I and III, and his father of Act II. Throughout the second act, in which we enter Michelín's innermost consciousness, we are made aware of the establishment of a very close symbolic relationship between the child and his father. This, in turn, leads us to perceive strong similarities in the life pattern of each one.

One of the strongest relationships develops out of Mercedes' destruction of the large *quenepo* that had once stood on the terrace, and of her similar destruction of Michel's manuscripts, which were his only hope of creating a future for himself after his release from prison. Michel's words exemplify the importance of the tree and of the manuscripts in both lives. He says of Michelín's fondness for the tree: "Pero en su soledad nuestro hijo había hecho de él un compañero, un confidente, un . . . protector" (139). Of his own manuscripts, he says: "La única esperanza que me quedaba. . . . El único asidero. . . . ¡Qué destrucción tan total!" (141). In neither case was either father or son capable of preventing the obliteration of his last security. And, in both cases, Mercedes, representative of the materiialistic world, is the person responsible for the total destruction of hope.

The accumulation of such parallels leads us to perceive the similar life patterns of Michelín and of his father. The father comes from a past whose history is tied to France and to Puerto Rico during a period when his own father and grandfather were also searching for freedom. Those past worlds were not really Michel's own, however, as he is a man of thoughts, not of action, as Thomas Feeny points out ("Woman's Triumph over Man in René Marqués, Theater" 188). His own future lies in the Bowery of New York where he dies an alcoholic. Michelín's past consists of a father who was in prison for most of his son's life, a mother who has adopted foreign values, and of Cecilia— raised a sister to Michel—who offers the child an attractive set of values related to his father's family and to past tradition, but which prove to be false because Michelín, as an individual, has no place in that world. The final correspondence in the similar life patterns comes with death. The father destroys himself with alcohol while the son destroys himself with another liquid—the poison used to kill the tree. Both die a lonely death, the only difference being that the father leaves a son—a sign of optimism for the future—, but the son leaves no hope for a future at all.

In the Puerto Rican colonial world, and in the family, controlled by Mercedes' materialism, Michelín's father's ideals of individual freedom, though noble ones, are unable to create a meaningful life for either father or son, except in death. Carlos Solórzano generalizes this idea as follows: "El antagonismo entre la civilización actual y el deseo de libertad individual, que constituye el tema central de todo el teatro de la posguerra, cobra en esta obra perfiles de crueldad extrema" (*Teatro latinoamericano en el siglo XX* 159-60). In the case of the father and of the son, the anguish resulting from the failure to liberate oneself motivates a painful and a solitary death. Although father and son rep- resent two generations—normally a sign of forward movement in time—, their parallel life patterns in which failures repeat themselves and ideals are lost, indicate the incidents of time to be repetitive and non-progressive.

The play's actual structure in which the present of Acts I and III in fact surrounds the past of Act II provides the key to the definitive establishment of coetaneity within Michelín's world. According to Piri Fernández, the entire second act can be seen as "una continuación técnica del juego de Michelín en escena" ("Temas del teatro puertorriqueño" 163). That game is what Michelín calls "playing the past," in which he enters into a dream-like realm, conjuring up images and events from an earlier time. The end of Act I and the beginning of Act III find him on the terrace in that dream-like state, implying that all of the events of the second act occur within that same condition. The penetration into the interior of the house in Act II, which takes place in the living room, suggests the invasion of Michelín's innermost consciousness.

The interiorization into Michelín's dream world occurs on two levels: that of the game in which he himself evokes the past, seemingly at will; and that of a deep sleep, in which the audience perceives on stage what supposedly is happening inside of the child's mind. In the former case, Michelín is somewhat in control of his own suffering (for instance, as he painfully feels the tree's death). On this level, he consciously elicits the help of Cecilia in playing the game, and even reveals his pastime to his friend Andrés. We understand the latter, however, to be his unshared dream world, of which the game is only a symptom. In the words of Piri Fernández, Michelín "rehace los momentos del pasado a su antojo, trocando así a la realidad en sombras, y, en cambio, convirtiendo a las sombras de su imaginación en sus más preciadas realidades" (162). His game of "playing the past" is, in Michelín's way, a solution to the problems with which he is confronted in Act II, since it is through this pastime on the superficial level that he can transform the present into a world with which he can cope.

Even though Michelín is not visibly present throughout much of Act II, the author subtly makes his presence known as the past events unfold, which Holzapfel points out ("In Search of Form and Identity" 157). Through the child's subtle presence, the audience observes the events *with* Michelín and at the same time, sees those same events as he previously has witnessed them. In the tense encounter between the parents in which the father accuses the mother of having brought about his own destruction, physically mistreats her, and then leaves the family definitively, we see Michelín's hand on the staircase. Interspersed throughout the parents' conversation the author's stage directions describe the effect: "(La mano de MICHELIN aparece en la pared del recodo alto de la escalera.)"—and "(Tras la mano de MICHELIN empieza a aparecer parte de su cuerpo, de espaldas a nosotros, muy pegado a la pared, como si quisiera incrustarse en ella. . .)" (141). Because of the child's presence, this key scene does not exist primarily to disclose details of the plot to the audience, but rather to reveal the nature of Michelín's past as a part of his inner present.

Michelín's reaction to the scene he has witnessed pulls together the images of circularity and entrapment prevalent throughout the play. He descends the stairs, in the author's words, "como si, de súbito, el buen Dios hubiese puesto una carga de siglos sobre sus espaldas" (142). He then tries to leave, but cannot. He goes to the hall by which his father left only to find this exit seemingly guarded by the full-length painting of his mother. He then runs to the glass door leading to the terrace but stops as if that exit, too, were closed to him. Motivated by all that he has learned from his parents' conversation, he attempts to escape from that burden of knowledge which he has acquired. However, he is trapped not only physically but emotionally as well, making escape impossible. This feeling of being trapped forms the child's inner world and prevents him from developing positive tactics to survive his present exterior world.

The play's coetaneity indicates the dual-level crisis which Michelín personifies as well as the heroic aspects of the child, who becomes the sacrificial victim of the world of conflicts in which he lives. Caught betwen the libertarian ideals of his father and the materialistic world of his mother, Michelín's personal conflict involves the suffocation of his own creative potential. Both value systems, at the same time, are intricately tied to the family's past and to Puerto Rico's history as a colony, first of Spain and later of the United States. These historical connections bring in the second level of the crisis, that of political freedom. On this larger scale, Michelín's conflict is that of the Puerto Rican island, caught between a search for individual identity and a materialistic world which gradually destroys the possibility of finding, or of developing, that identity.

In his treatise on human existence, Jean Paul Sartre claimed: "At my limit, at that infinitesimal instant of my death, I shall be no more than my past. It alone will define me" (*Being and Nothingness* 91). In this same spirit, Michelin's death gives him an indelible identity, as the fusion of past, present and future into one instant invests meaning into the child's suicide. The spectator realizes he is witnessing an approximation of the psychological time and state-of-mind of the protagonist.

Michelín's age, his natural opposition to Andrés, and the ritual with which he is associated reveal him to be a symbolic representative of the future, a learning experience personified, and an expiatory victim (see Villegas) of the present world in which he lives. The fact that this protagonist is a child is significant in itself, inasmuch as children in general, on a symbolic level, represent the future of their own society.

The natural opposition which Marqués creates between Michelín and his guest, Andrés, provides another clue to the protagonist's symbolic nature. Michelín's intelligence, intellectual maturity, sensitivity, and his poetic tendencies contrast to the personal qualities of Andrés, who is of lesser intelligence and lacks sensitivity, and is therefore incapable of understanding Michelín's game of the past. In the author's stage directions, he says: "ANDRES será, sin duda, en los años por venir, un hombre sabiamente pegado a la tierra; un ciudadano intachable, hasta un funcionario probo, pero jamás un ser humano en quien el género pueda experimentar una experiencia heroicamente aleccionadora" (74). In view of the series of contrasts established between the two, this statement suggests that Michelín *is* a person through whom the human race can experience a "heroic" enlightenment.

Furthermore, nearly every action which Michelín initiates during the course of the play is of a ritualistic nature. Michelín's game of the past in which he forces Cecilia to paticipate is indicative of the ritual. First of all, he and Cecilia each take specific positions: she, near the door to the house and he, on the trellis, assuming the position of a crucified victim. There are next certain words which are uttered to the rhythm of violin music: "El niño estaba en el árbol y dijo: '¡Odiame viento y azótame la cara!' (*Sube suavemente la música*) Pero el viento estaba lejos, inflando la vela púrpura de un pescador en el mar. Y el árbol estaba inmóvil como si fuese de piedra. Y el niño estaba en la rama pensando en el árbol muerto" (88). The chanted nature and the solitary meaning of his words indicate his isolation and state of helplessness. At the same time, the evoked ritual underlines the fact that this is no child's game, but rather a most solemn ceremony. He approaches his other actions in a like manner. For example, after the "assassination" of the statue, he explains symbolically each of the designs he painted on the standard bearer of liberty. Likewise, his own act of suicide, paralleling the game of the tree's assassination, is of a symbolic nature, with the exception that this time it is not a game, and Michelín himself takes the place of the tree. As a result of these rites with which Michelín is associated, he becomes the "niño- ofrenda," as Juan Villegas refers to him ("Los motivos en *Un niño azul para esa sombra* 93).

Michelín is the representative of his own society whose potential is exemplified in that of a child on the verge of manhood. He stands for a society, however, trapped in a state of non-progress, between the conflicting ideals of U. S. materialism and a quest for freedom and individuality. On a symbolic level, he projects a conflict in which Puerto Rico's own identity and potential might become a victim like Michelín, or might be saved because of the lesson to be learned from his example.

The play's coetaneity defines Michelín's identity which, in turn, symbolizes that of Marqués' Puerto Rico. The play's events, including those of the past, coexist in the present time: Acts I and III are the actual present while the past occurrences which Act II portrays are Michelín's present inner reality. The coexistence of past and present in these dimensions restricts the child's identity to a cycle in which his inner reality forms the basis for the way in which he reacts to the present events acting on him. Until the play's end, his identity does not surpass this action-reaction cycle. He performs a heroic act upon choosing suicide as a response to his dilemma because, in this case, the only freedom open to the child is that of making this particular choice. His death is an ironic event (like that of Emilia and Inés) in that at the same time it is heroic and serves as a learning experience for the audience, it implies no future at all for the play's ill-fated protagonist.

Michelín's death becomes a message which demonstrates the dimensions of the conflict which the play portrays. In the terms of the play, this conflict is a struggle in which the "status quo" relationship with the United States signals the death of cultural identity and political progress for the island of Puerto Rico, and in which materialistic ideals signal the destruction of artistic creativity and philosophical progress on the level of the individual.

While the establishment of coexisting spatial and temporal dimensions is different in each of these two works, the end results are quite similar. In *Los soles truncos*, the various dimensions of space and time dramatically interact until the two sisters arrive at a point of decision. At one and the same time, however, it is clear that the sisters' inner conflicts based on guilt, jealousy, and hatred, are in part responsible for their having created an inner space in which to survive. Those same conflicts are the cause as well for the antagonism between their own and the world outside. They are not solely at fault for their destiny, however, because time is almost a personified being whose passage contributes to the conflicts and over whom the Burkharts have no control.

Time, in *Un niño azul para esa sombra*, has been such a force, but when the play opens, has already exercised its power. The multiple dimensions of time and space here exist within the child-protagonist. The worlds within his house and outside of it, as well as his past experiences, exert pressure on the inner, psychological world he has created for himself until his reclusion no longer protects him; and he, as do the Burkharts, chooses suicide as the only solution.

In both of these works, however, the coetaneous and contiguous configurations of space and time reveal the same dual-natured conflict: on the socio-political level, the materialistic world of the U. S. imposes a cultural identity upon Puerto Rico incompatible with its cultural past, while on the personal level, the individuals involved cannot resolve their own human nature with all of its shortcomings and/or strengths to the demands made upon them by the socio-political conflict.

Chapter IV

Rhythm and Virtual Space

The two plays, *La carreta* (1951) and *Carnaval afuera, carnaval adentro* (1960) are distant from one another in years and seemingly in their respective presentations. *La carreta* is presented in extremely realistic settings and events, inspired by the mass emigrations from the Island in the late forties. *Carnaval afuera, carnaval adentro*, on the other hand, is presented in an absurdist vein, using many techniques related to the European "Theatre of the Absurd," but not actually entering that realm. A close examination of these plays reveals a common origin for the dynamics of each work in the development of dramatic rhythm and the creation of virtual space. The sense of space and rhythm which each work creates is the very basis of communication of the plays' major themes and postures.

La carreta was the first of René Marqués' dramatic creations to bring him enthusiastic critical acclaim. Indeed, the well-respected critic María Teresa Babín has said that this play "is worthy of figuring among the best works of all of Latin American theatre" (prologue to *La carreta* VI). The fact that *La carreta* is one of the most-often performed of Marqués works speaks to its dramatic appeal and universality. The three-act play depicts the story of a rural Puerto Rican family, who, at the insistence of the older son, leaves the traditional way of life to search for better social and economic conditions in the mechanized, industrial life of the city. Acts One, Two, and Three correspond respectively in time and place to: 1) the poor country shack in the mountains; 2) the makeshift hut in the San Juan district of La Perla; and 3) the sixth-floor walk-up apartment in the Bronx, New York.

The theatrical space which any play creates is related to the concept of what Susanne Langer calls "virtual space." To explain the concept, she uses the example of the space created in a painting, which is organized by color and shapes. This space exists only because of the arrangement of colors and shapes on a given canvas (*Feeling and Form*

72). Were the canvas to be destroyed, the space created in the painting's scene would cease to be and could never be re-created exactly as it was. In Langer's view, the painting's illusory space is a "virtual" one. The staging of a play creates space in a similar way. Upon the real place of the stage, objects, characters, lighting, sound, and any other elements present, create an illusory space that ceases to exist at the end of the performance. Because the space which a dramatic work creates is three-dimensional as well as pictorial, virtual space in the theatre also includes the creation of a certain *ambiance*. The vital feeling which belongs within the virtual space of a particular play is similar to that created in an architectural structure, such as a house for example. This space is "the created domain of human relations and activities" and, like the pictorial space, is an illusion, since the "atmosphere" disappears when the structure is significantly altered or is destroyed (Langer 99).

René Marqués' *La carreta* derives its dynamism from a virtual space that is both pictorial and architectural. The play carries the subtitle "Tres estampas boricuas" and is, in a figurative sense, an engraving in which each act imprints visually and experientially for the spectator a different scene in the changing life of *this* Puerto Rican family. The specific setting of each act is the family's living quarters, in which objects take on significance past their contribution to the staging, as they continually serve as a reminder of another life style. The word *boricuas* of the subtitle (meaning literally, Puerto Rican) signifies the vital feeling which dominates the three scenes, each of which offers René Marqués' view of the disintegration of what is Puerto Rican in the life of these particular characters. The diminishing boriicuan ambiance from one act to the next transforms the play from being exclusively a *costumbrista* work into one with universal subtleties in which two conflicting life styles are embodied in the lives of the characters. Their conflict is not the more simply stated one between the past and present, nor is it a plea for a return to the past; but rather, it is a conflict which develops from two co-existing ways of approaching life in the face of the particular crises of the period it depicts. As the tension between the two visions grows into open conflict, the characters are forced into a dramatic resolution which creates hope for their own future.

Time in the play interacts with the virtual space to create dramatic movement within each act and within the whole work. Against this spatial background it indicates the destruction direction in which the family is heading as the traditional rhythm of their life is broken, so that each act reflects not only the changing physical conditions and superficial relationships, but the deeper emotional ones as well. First, time manifests itself as part of the theme. This aspect is the chronological ordering that makes up the experience we call past, present, and future and whose underlying principle is change (Langer 112). That same principle applies to the linear time in *La carreta* as we see the family at three successive moments, whose juxtaposition simultaneously implies temporal movement, as well as the changes that have occurred between one episode and the next.

Second, the time-related element known as tempo creates an experiential link between the play and the audience. According to J. L. Styan, tempo in a dramatic work is the the certain speed in time in which dramatic impressions follow one another in a related sequence (*The Elements of Drama* 41), and "it [tempo] always exists to evoke meaning" (41). In *La carreta*, changing tempo from one act to the next makes the spectator aware of a repeated pattern of disintegration of the traditional life. While linear time indicates change, and tempo conveys the experience of disintegration, physical objects in each act symbolize the transformations that take place from year to year while simultaneously those same objects serve to point out the tempo of life at each stage.

The virtual space and vital feeling, which each stage setting creates, reflect the disintegrating rhythm of the play as well as of the way of life of the rural Puerto Rican who, as presented by Marqués in this play, has abandoned his land. In the first act, the economic and cultural conflict is evident from the beginning, in the stage setting and in the values of the characters, especially of Don Chago and of Luis. The tempo is slow and drawn out, and despite the activity of the moving preparations, not much happens, an indication of the pace of life in the rural setting. The setting of Act One is the interior of a country house made of "buenas maderas del país, como restos de una época de mejor situación económica, remendada con pichipén y retazos de madera barata importada" (*La carreta* 4). Thus, the appearance of the house, against a background of a more desirable past, tells a story of the worsening economic conditions from which the family is fleeing.

Each of the family members represents a slightly different position on a scale of values, with Don Chago, the patriarch, and Luis, the oldest son, at the two extremes. Don Chago's view of life sees the dollar and "progress" as having taken the place of human dignity. While he does present the past as a better way of life, what Don Chago ultimately stands for is not so much the physical style of living as the spiritual involvement and responsibility of the people in their style of life. Luis, however, has a different opinion of where a person's involvement should lie. He is also concerned about the loss of dignity, but his concern is related to what he sees as a hierarchical social status in which progress has to do with upward mobility. He associates a "better life" with more money, and in turn, having more money with a more highly regarded social status. The play's development moves the family away from Don Chago's side of the scale towards Luis', and then back again, making a full circle at the work's end.

The tension grows throughout the act but becomes explicit through the image of the oxcart. Near the end of this act, the sound of the oxcart's turning wheels interrupts the nostalgic scene in which the family enjoys their final cup of coffee together, and makes the confrontation with the present problem imminent. At the first sound, the characters become immobile for an instant, giving the audience time to reflect on the meaning contained in this scene. The stage directions describe the play's ambiance as follows: "Sobre ellos pasa una gran sombra de angustia, una muda interrogación al futuro, un miedo al mañana, un deseo de no actuar, de permanecer allí clavados y dejar que pase de largo la fascinación de la carreta" (44). In this manner, the idea of the oxcart (for it never appears on stage) juxtaposed to the long, slow nostalgic scene communicates to the viewer the importance of this moment which represents a crossroad of life for these people.

The second act, taking place one year later, finds the family located in San Juan between the old fortress wall and the ocean, in *La Perla*. Despite Luis' dream of a more comfortable life for the family, the fact that there has been no improvement in their economic status is readily apparent. Moreover, this Puerto Rican family is embroiled in the cultural conflict between the old and the new ways of life at which the first act only hints. The economic and cultural contention is revealed in the stage setting as it contrasts to the house of the past; in the changing values and bitterness of each of the characters; in the now frenzied tempo which creates a sensation of dizziness; and in the tension which the constant presence of a rocking chair brought from the country creates visually. These dramatic elements highlight the development of the play's implicit meaning which the various contrasts and changes, together with the frenetic tempo, create.

The curtain opens onto an empty stage, thus allowing time for the audience to experience the disparities to which the stage setting itself contributes. Because of the arrangement of the house in La Perla, the spectator immediately perceives a clear similarity to the former house in the country. The material of which the house is constructed, however, is in opposition to the country home, which, although it has a rundown appearance due to the attempts at repair, is made of "good wood from the island" and therefore has a strong basic construction. Antithetically, the house in La Perla gives a precarious appearance because it lacks a solid foundation and is nothing more than an accumulation of unmatched, discarded non-durable type materials. In the brief moment at the beginning when the stage is empty, the audience has the opportunity to perceive the obvious economic and cultural changes which have taken place, and to become aware of the growing disillusionment throughout the act which causes the disintegration of the family's intimate relationships with each other as well as that of each individual's personal values.

Throughout this act the value system of each family member is threatened and while not totally destroyed, at least diminished in the face of the new crises which confront each character and which bring the family to one of the lowest points of morale. Chaguito, the youngest son, is the first to succumb to the city life as he is caught and imprisoned for stealing money from tourists while trying to sell them the San Antonio statue he had stolen from his own mother. Doña Gabriela's daughter, Juanita, is raped and reluctantly agrees to an abortion and then attempts suicide. Luis' plight at first seems to have improved, as he has finally found a job and has many plans for the future. However, he, too, becomes disillusioned as the way of life destroys *his* dreams one by one. Doña Gabriela, through all of her family's tragedies, holds on to her father's ideals of "digniá y vergüensa," but she, too, finally gives up, leaving Luis to make the final decision about the future.

The rhythm of this act that serves as background to these crises is the final dramatic element that combines with the setting and actual events to convey the characters' experience of desperation to the audience. Various sounds as well as the frenzy of activity and ups and downs in tension convey to the spectator a dizzying tempo. The focus of this act is on the actual experience of the characters, surrounded by a way of life to which they have no means of adapting. Sounds associated rhythmically with the action figure prominently in the experience of vertigo as the characters search for a direction to follow. The first of these sounds is that of a jukebox whose harsh music does not blend with what remains of the vital boricuan feeling within the family home. What the spectator perceives visually is a house resembling the old one. Experientially, the viewer perceives the stark contrast between the jukebox music and the solitude on stage. Throughout this act, the music penetrates at key moments from the outside until it becomes an intruder over which the family has no control.

The change in the rhythm of life between the first act and the second is most clearly obvious at the moment when Juanita opens a hand-carved replica of the oxcart which her former boyfriend sends to her. The sight of the gift evokes the way of life left behind as Juanita lifts up the oxcart and the spectator hears the words, as if from Juanita's memories, of the oxcart driver. Those words are then drowned out by the sound of an airplane. In this scene, we find Juanita symbolically and emotionally torn between Don Chago's world, which the oxcart evokes, and her brother Luis' world for which the airplane stands. As the sound of the plane drowns out the sounds of Juanita's memories, we are reminded of the changing pace and of the lost values. Significantly, each of these sounds communicates meaning when examined as an integral part of the whole act. Each sound has a rhythm of its own and the variety of rhythms as well as the quantity of different tempos work with the rapid scene changes and variety of happenings to convey the experience of frenzied movement which seems to bring only negative results.

The presence of the rocking chair brought from the old house serves as the focal point, physically and spiritually, of the cultural crises which the family undergoes in this act. Because of the contrast it offers to the rest of the furnishings, the chair becomes a constant visual reminder of the life left behind. Moreover, its position in the center of the room makes it symbolic of the central place the former life still maintains within the family nucleus. The rocking motion contrasts directly with the frenzy of the world revolving around the chair and reflects the differences in values as well as in the pace of life. Throughout this act, the rocking chair's central position on stage constantly reminds both audience and characters of the cultural (and personal) tensions at work in this dramatized world.

The last scene of act two brings together the differing life styles and creates a second crossroads revealing the further disintegration of the family and of its ideals. Here the juxtaposition of the rocking chair to the sounds of the jukebox music communicates the downward direction in which the family is heading. Each one in his or her own way tries to escape the problem without really facing it: Chaguito by stealing; Juanita by attempting to end her life; Doña Gabriela by rocking and going nowhere, and all have failed to change or alleviate their worsening situation. Only Luis is left to impose *his* way of escaping, which is to go, by plane, to New York.

The third act shows both economic and cultural changes. The absence of the once traditional way of life is evident in the stage setting as well as in the supposed values and in the characters' physical appearance. The stage setting, so totally different from the first two, offers almost no link to the past. The Bronx apartment reveals both poverty and foreignness as we compare this home to the two previous ones. The arrangement of the room has no similarity to the previous stage settings and many aspects suggest isolation and distance, physically as well as culturally, from the original rural setting. Not the least of these is the fact that the apartment is on the sixth floor, vertically adding distance to that between the family and their homeland. In addition, the presence of a steam heater and heavy winter clothing, uncommon sights in the Puerto Rican past, also lend a certain foreign aura to the surroundings.

Changes in the physical appearance of the characters reflect transformations in their personal values as well as in their family relationships. Ironically, the cause of the changes comes from the fact that, although the family's economic condition is much improved over the previous acts, their spiritual and emotional well-being has deteriorated to the point of making them either bitter, as in the case of Juanita, or desperate, as is Luis. Juanita's choice to move away from her family and isolate herself from them reflects the tendency of the Puerto Ricans in this particular play to go in separate directions, so that the family, which once moved together, no longer has a unity with which to face the strange new life.

In the first few moments of this act, sounds and rhythms set the tempo as well as reflect the play's direction and *denouement*. The syncopated and fragmented tempo here at times becomes a violent and destructive force at work in the lives of these characters. As the curtain opens onto the empty stage, the sounds of a jackhammer and of an elevated train enter through the window. These rhythms, together with those of blues music heard a few minutes later, blend with the various forms of fragmentation prevalent throughout the act as well as with the characters' lack of direction in their lives. However, after this first impression, the well-known Puerto Rican *danza* "Margarita," replaces the blues music, an indication of Juanita's progressive awareness and definite decision, and a suggestion, in a subliminal way, of the final direction she and her mother will take.

In addition to conflicts within the family group and evidence of the adulteration of their language, which takes on many anglicisms in this act, the most significant relators of the tempo are the varied events which involve people from outside the family. These events suggest the possible avenues which the Puerto Rican might follow and together form a chaotic world whose roads lead either to unhappiness or to physical destruction. Such incidents indicate the chaos surrounding the protagonist-family, while simultaneously, the lives of Luis and Juanita take on specific directions. Luis, motivated by his fascination for the industrialized society's machines, holds stubbornly to his dream of progress. Throughout the act, and despite his feeling of unrest and disappointment, Luis follows the course he has set for himself even before the play begins, a course which costs him his life as the machine that attracts him, in the end, destroys him. Juanita's own direction begins to take form and finally, through the lesson she recognizes in Luis' death, the play's message becomes clear, unity is restored to the family, and hope for regaining the lost spiritual relationship between man and his homeland once more seems possible.

Just prior to news of Luis' death, Doña Gabriela reveals what the play has clearly suggested from the start—that Luis was neither her son nor her husband's. Although some critics have objected to this relationship, it seems quite relevant when taken as part of the ultimate message hinted at throughout the play. Doña Gabriela reveals this final part of the lesson to her daughter as follows: "Pero Luis siempre ha sío un huéfano. ¿No te dah cuenta que se la pasa buhcando, como un cabrito perdío que no encuentra a su madre?" (162). At this point, Luis becomes a symbol of that Puerto Rican who, according to René Marqués, is an orphan because he does not recognize where to look for his parent, but rather, follows blindly the direction set by foreign values and ways of life.

Through Luis' sacrifice Juanita, with her new knowledge, imposes the final order on the play as she makes of the oxcart the symbol of the "correct" (according to the playwright) direction one should follow. Juanita's famous words reveal her new knowledge and strength:

Porque no eh cosa de volver a la tierra pa vivir como muertoh. Ahora sabemos que el mundo no cambia por sí mihmo. Que somoh nosotroh loh que cambiamoh al mundo. Y vamoh a ayudar a cambiarlo. Vamoh a dir como gente con digniá, como desía el abuelo. Con la cabesa muy alta. (172)

Finally in Luis' death, Juanita has learned the meaning of what her grandfather said when the family left their home and what Doña Gabriela repeats. That is, the land has the capacity to nurture and to give dignity and respect to its people, but that those people must recognize their responsibility to return their own love and respect to that land in exchange.

La carreta presents three separate visual and experiential impressions which convey the dramatically conceived "vital feeling" of the conflictive Puerto Rican life. The play's virtual space and disintegrating rhythms communicate to the spectator the spiritual losses within a system that, in the dramatist's view, is attempting to reconcile its cultural heritage with a changing life style. In the work's development, as the family becomes more and more torn apart physically and spiritually, the remaining members come to an awareness that only by accepting the legacy of their Puerto Rican heritage while simultaneously fulfilling their responsibility to their native land can they maintain intact their spiritual integrity.

Carnaval afuera, carnaval adentro, written in 1960, was not published until 1971, and did not premiere in Puerto Rico in a professional production until April 14, 1983, although there was a non-professional staging of it in July, 1972. The play's world premier took place in Havana during the Latin American Theatre Festival of 1962, the year in which the play also received honorable mention in the *Casa de las Américas'* theatre competition. Although Marqués had submitted this work to the Institute of Culture's Annual Puerto Rican Theatre Festival in 1960, the play was not chosen, for political reasons according to Marqués. If what Marqués' believed is true, the Institute's censors did not read deeply enough into the work. While the play does openly criticize the absolute economic and political power which the United States holds over the Island, it also criticizes the Puerto Rican people for succumbing to that power and accuses them as accomplices in the destruction of cultural and universal human values. Indeed, this latter point is the very basis of the play.

In *Carnaval afuera, carnaval adentro*, Marqués utilizes techniques from the theatre of the absurd to portray the sacrifice of both cultural and human authenticity as his characters compromise themselves to the consumerism of the modern world. The work, however, as Daniel Zalacaín has said, does not belong to the European theatre of the absurd, but rather, is "absurdist." According to Zalacaín: "Mientras que los dramaturgos del absurdo miran la realidad como un círculo cerrado, Marqués ve en ella una abertura. Su posición como artista comprometido con la realidad social de Puerto Rico no le permite seguir la filosofía de derrota que trata el 'teatro del absurdo.' Sin embargo, en lo referente a la técnica, Marqués hace marcado uso de técnicas derivadas de este teatro; por esa razón se debe denominar la obra del dramaturgo absurdista, en vez de absurda" ("René Marqués, del absurdo a la realidad" 35). In addition, unlike those works usually associated with the "theatre of the absurd," this play does leave an opening for a hopeful future as the character Angel, champion of love, art, and liberty, is freed in order to continue the fight for those disappearing values.

Tía Matilde is the character of free will who directs the others as if she were a circus trainer. Each character, with the exception of Tía Matilde, is a puppet/caricature which symbolizes human qualities, both negative and positive. Doña Rosa represents Puerto Rican culture and tradition and in the end becomes the Attorney for the Defense while Rosita, alias Rosie, symbolizes innocence, ultimately to be sacrificed in order to save the meaningful values which Angel represents. Other characters represent negative qualities such as automation (Felícita), consumerism (Guillermo, alias Willie and María, alias Mary), and commercialism (El Apoderado and don Mack). Yet others are stereotypical of persons who might be found in an elite gathering or party on the Island: La Condesa and her nephew, Rasputo, Cuban refugees; George, a North American who resides on the tropical island; and Pito Jilguera, a Latin American diplomat. In the last act, stripped of their hypocrital façade, these characters become respectively, a Medieval Judge, a Puritan Pilgrim, a Bishop, and a Latin American dictator. Brandishing a whip and dressed as an animal trainer, Tía Matilde exerts complete control over characters and actors alike and becomes the pivotal point through which the work overflows into the world of the audience. Besides her more practical role of director, she fulfills a symbolic role as the life force which unites the Puerto Rican culture, personified in the character Doña Rosa, and the universal values which the artist Angel represents.

That this work of René Marqués belongs to the world of metatheatre is evident in the use of the carnival masquerade which the
play's title suggests. In the book *Metatheatre*, Lionel Abel defines that
term as a theatrical phenomenon based on two principles: "the world
is a stage, life is a dream" (79). This highly stylized play is designed
constantly to remind the spectator that what he/she is viewing is *acted*
theatre with no attempt to create an aura of realism as in *La carreta*.
From the carnival outside, the play progresses to the social farce
within the house, climaxing in the unmasking of the inner personal
motives of the characters.

By the creation of a *carnavalada*, or a joke reminiscent of those
played during carnival, the author directs himself to the audience in
order that the spectator might see that the falseness represented on
stage is simply a reflection of that same condition in the viewer. In so
doing, Marqués emphasizes the Shakespearean idea to which Abel
refers, that all the world's a stage. Abel goes on to say, especially in
relation to Brechtian theatre, that "in the main it is by the fact that they
are capable of feeling pain that others proclaim their reality to us, and
by sympathizing with their feelings we in fact maintain their reality"
(106). Conversely, when one perceives no feeling or "inner necessity"
in the characters, their world is a dream world. In this sense, the
characters of Marqués' play live in a dream world for they do not ever
seem real to us nor do they portray any deep emotions to each other.
Furthermore, Tía Matilde, Doña Rosa, and Angel are conscious of the
fact that they are all acting roles. Through the carnivalesque recourse
the audience, too, becomes aware of its own role-playing in the real life
outside of the play.

The play dramatizes an unusual business transaction in which
Rosita, who personifies innocence, is to be sold to Mack, the absolute
power which controls the puppet/characters, and as revealed later, a
cannibal. This later, absent character explicitly symbolizes the negative influence of United States consumerism on Puerto Rico. Before
Rosita is turned over to Mack, she falls in love with the artist Angel,
champion of art, liberty and love—attributes which are lacking in the
world of the puppet/characters of the work. Rosita loses her virginity
to Angel at the end of the second act, and this motivates the trial by jury
in the third in which Angel is condemned to death. However, before
the execution is carried out, Tía Matilde exchanges Angel for Rosita.
The other characters are ignorant of the exchange and proceed to
assassinate Rosita in a grotesque ritual. Without doubt, the play

establishes the superiority of traditional values over those of the consumer world resulting from Puerto Rico's colonial existence. The work achieves universality as it delves into the innermost motivations of the characters, who sacrifice the authentic values of love, liberty, and art in favor of don Mack's materialism.

The work's structural development depends on the unmasking of the interior world of the characters. The carnival trick creates a direct link between the farce portrayed on stage and the real life of the audience. An unsettling rhythm in several scenes suppresses the normal flow of time. The dramatic spaces reflect back and forth upon each other to conclude that the real farce is carried out within the spectator. Techniques borrowed from the theatre of the absurd such as the circus atmosphere, the clichés, and the superficial conversations, together with the carnivalesque rhythm that takes the place of normal time, create in this work a world without authentic human values.

This play is comprised of three dramatic spaces: first, the visible dramatized world located in a restored, colonial house in Old San Juan; second, the offstage world in which the carnival preceding lent is taking place; and, third, the house where the audience is seated. In the end, this third space becomes an extension of the world which the play portrays. According to Stanley Vincent Longman, the worlds of a theatrical work operate for the public on three levels of perception: "the actual activity (actors acting); the imagined activity (characters living); the interior world (audience experiencing vicariously)" ("The Spatial Dimension of Theatre" 47). Using Longman's theory as a starting point, we can see how Marqués creates a sense of space and rhythm that leads us through the various levels of perception to the end when the farce is directed towards the audience, which in turn becomes aware of the theatrical quality in "real" life.

On the first level—the visible world of the play—everything is masked, thus suggesting a hidden reality. For example, the restored house in Old San Juan in which the action develops, has a masked reality confirmed by the attempts to disguise the past life of the house. The obvious restoration attempts disguise but do not totally hide its age or its original appearance. We can observe a similar process in the names, the clothing, and the rhythmical action, which all together create an infinite mirror effect. The names "María, alias Mary" and "Guillermo, alias Willie," denote the conflict caused by the North American influence on the Puerto Rican culture. The carnival from outside enters this level of the play in the black and white costumes of the *vegigantes* who come in at the end of the first act. The last scene of Act I is repeated as the first scene of the second act much like an "instant replay," but with a variation that implies a symbolic meaning. There appear in that scene *vegigantes* who, through a menacing ritual, symbolically accuse and condemn the characters who have just arranged to sell Rosita to Mack. The black and white costumes of these *vegigantes* are later reflected in the dresses of the Condesa, the Viuda del Huérfano, and, again, in Act III, in the costumes of the Cinco Máscaras Negras, thus serving as a reminder throughout the play of the *vegigantes'* early accusation.

From the very first moment, a chaotic rhythm replaces the normal flow of time. The opening scene establishes tension between the two rhythms of the work. In this first scene in which we hear only sounds from a dark stage, we perceive from offstage the sounds of a traffic jam evidently created by a *paso fino* horse whose steps sound "rítmicamente sobre los adoquines centenarios" (23). The dramatist's stage directions indicate the presence of the two rhythms: "sube ensordecedor el coro de *claxons*. Inexplicablemente, por encima de todo el barullo, ha seguido sonando el rítmico golpear de los cascos del caballo sobre los adoquines" (24). The horse's trotting and the sound of the car horns (the former representative of the Island's history and the latter of today's consumer society) mirror the tension between the two temporal elements and establish the tempo in which the play is to develop.

Language and the movements of the characters also reflect the rhythm of the traffic jam, and doing so, impose an aura of superficiality on all that the characters say and do. This is especially evident in the play's opening scene when the maid, Felícita, enters. This character moves and speaks as if imitating a locomotive, and she never has anything of substance to say. She comes in saying "tut-tut, tut, tut, tut-tut" (28) moving in time to the rhythm her words create. She answers the phone and maintains the same rhythm throughout the one-sided conversation, as follows:

> Automotor de las ocho. Dos minutos de retraso. Rosie no está. O no sé si está. Ni me importa *na*. ¿En Caribe Beach? (*En falsete.*) Bich-bich-bich. (*Natural*.) ¿Canasta? Banasta, lacasta, papastra, mamastra. . . . Sí, don Mack. No, don Mack. Sí, don Mack. (*En falsete.*). Troc mac, macac, cucac, tracacacac. . . . (28)

Her short sentences and the nonsense she speaks, as well as the rhythm in which she speaks, not only reflect the chaos of the traffic jam from before, but foreshadow conversations between all of those characters who will ultimately be accused of Rosita's death.

The entrance of Rosita, alias Rosie, reflects the superficiality and chaotic rhythm which Felícita establishes. The representative of innocence enters the scene with an earth-shattering scream as she slides down the bannister. Dancing to rock 'n' roll music, the only words she utters are "Mack. Mack. Mack" (30). The author's stage directions specify that the music be "el último baile desarticulado que exporta Norteamérica a la fecha de realizarse la producción" (30). Significantly, Angel enters through the window, turns off the music, and speaks in a totally normal way, thus providing a stark contrast to the frenzy that exists within the house.

The rhythm which the horse's steps imply is repeated at the end of the second act in the love scene between Rosita and Angel. As Rosita enters, the previous frenzy gives way to smooth and refined actions as reflected in her movements: "sus gestos y movimientos son ahora delicados, refinados, suavemente rítmicos" (83). The change in rhythm is also reinforced by the background music. What were sonorous drum beats is now smooth, delicate violin music. Once again we glimpse a different rhythm of life beneath the surface of activity.

The third level of perception, that of vicarious experience, develops within the courtroom of the final act. The room is the same one seen in the two previous acts but without furniture and adornment. The puppet/characters now are actors who interpret the caricaturesque roles of Medieval Judges, a Bishop, and a Latin American military governor or dictator. Characters named Las Cinco Máscaras Negras and La Viuda del Huérfano and dressed in black outfits similar to those worn by the Vegigantes surround the scene, creating the visual impression of an infernal world. In this environment, the characters reveal their interior motivations without disguising them.

A change of rhythm and a respite from the intensity signify the end of the rite and of the play. Under Tía Matilde's constant direction, the actors and actresses who are wearing masks begin to remove them on stage. Their uncovered faces are totally inexpressive, however, as are those of the characters who did not cover their faces at all. This complete lack of expression becomes yet another mask hiding the identity of the person behind it. In the final scene, which is a visually grotesque accusation directed at the audience, Angel establishes the relationship between the work and the spectators as he declares: "Para ustedes, ahí afuera, sigue el carnaval" (128). Tía Matilde makes the actors dance and laugh to a background of carnival music as if they were puppets and she the puppeteer. She assumes the role of play director and says: "¡La risa, actores, la risa de ellos! ¡La risa de carnaval para ellos!" (130). The actors respond with a soundless laughter so that their actions appear as grotesque facial contorsions. As each actor then salutes the audience, the resulting tension creates a mirror reflection through which the spectators experience the uneasy sensation of seeing themselves from the inside out. The carnivalesque world of the play embraces the spectators when they see that they, like the play's characters have sacrificed authentic human values in favor of a materialistic life.

In *Carnaval afuera, carnaval adentro*, René Marqués has created spatial and temporal dimensions which give depth to the play by establishing lines of tension between the work, the actors, the characters and the audience. Technically, Marqués becomes master of the most contemporary theatrical recourses of his day in order to expose his search for a true Puerto Rican identity. As he integrates technique and theme, he surpasses regional limits and carries his work to the universal level of questioning human existence. Throughout his works, Marqués is an author of high calibre who projects the Puerto Rican circumstance to a universal level.

These two seemingly diverse plays derive their dynamics from the way in which Marqués uses virtual space and dramatic rhythm. In *La carreta*, three separate impressions that are both visual and experiential convey the "vital feeling" of Puerto Rican life. The creation of this virtual space upon the stage couples with disintegrating rhythms to communicate the spiritual loss within a system that refuses (or does not know how) to recognize its cultural heritage. In the work's development, as the family becomes more and more disjointed physically and spiritually, the remaining members come to an awareness that only by fulfilling their responsibility towards their land and accepting the legacy of the past can they regain and maintain their spiritual integrity.

The same conflict between two incompatible lifestyles is at the center of *Carnaval afuera, carnaval adentro* in which the virtual space created on stage is shaped by materialistic values. Hidden beneath the visible scene is a world in which the more authentic values are hidden by disguises but do in fact exist. Each act progressively transforms the space from that of the living quarters of a family to a symbolic space which, when stripped of its masks, reveals the interior motives of the characters. Tension between a chaotic rhythm opposed to a smoothly flowing one further reinforces the conflict seen in the spatial dimensions.

In both works, René Marqués avails himself of the virtual Puerto Rican ambiance seen from two diverse vantage points, and the creation of conflictive rhythms to communicate the need of searching for a uniquely Puerto Rican identity and his belief in each individual's responsibility in that search.

Chapter V

History: Unfulfilled Fulfillment

In *La muerte no entrará en palacio* and *Mariana o el alba*, both clearly based on well-known historical events, Marqués makes history, as a recounting of the past, relevant to the present. In each of these plays the resolution of the work itself underscores the failure of the historical purposes and lays the responsibility for the continuing fight for those purposes at the feet of the present generation.

La muerte no entrará en palacio, written in 1956, is one of the best known and most volatile of Marqués' plays. Because of its overt political nature it has not yet been produced in Puerto Rico (private conversation with José Lacomba, Spring 1982). In this play, René Marqués creates a microcosmic world in which myth and reality fuse to create a semblance of history in virtual time and space. The use of characters with both a mythical and a theatrical past creates the perspective from which Marqués interprets the historical event of Luis Muñoz Marín's governorship of Puerto Rico and the signing of the Commonwealth agreement with the United States, an interpretation much in the spirit of the Mexican dramas of Rodolfo Usigli which he called "antihistories." Indeed, the words Marqués wrote in 1948 about Usigli's *Corona de sombra* apply equally well to Marqués' own *La muerte no entrará en palacio*:

> Si Maximiliano y Carlota existieron en un mundo real es algo que para los efectos del drama resulta secundario. . . . Si la realidad histórica coincide en ocasiones con la creación poética o si ésta tomó su inspiración de la realidad histórica son problemas que no interesan al teatro. *Corona de Sombra* es una obra dramática y como tal ha de juzgarse." ("Reseña: Usigli, Rodolfo" 98)

Because of the temporal proximity of Marqués' drama to the historical events which form its base, it is often difficult to separate the factual events from the dramatically created ones. No doubt, Marqués counted on this when he composed his work. The fact remains, however, that whether or not the characters coincide with their historical counterparts, *La muerte no entrará en palacio* is a powerful drama, creatively conceived in the best Marqués tradition.

As he does in most of his plays, Marqués parenthetically expands his title, which in this case is a "tragedia en dos actos y cuatro cuadros" (183). Frank Dauster, in his perceptive discussion of the theories of Francis Fergusson and Northrup Frye, suggests that the "tragic" rhythms and patterns are in actuality the rhythms of life and that the rhythm of tragedy and that of comedy are simply "variantes del ritmo vital de la acción psíquica" ("Hacia una teoría del teatro" 130). He goes on to say:

> La diferencia entre ellas en la vida cotidiana o en la literatura se halla en las diferencias que hay entre los distintos individuos y entre nuestras distintas maneras de reaccionar a los estímulos. . . . En fin, la distinción en la literatura es de punto de vista o de ángulo de perspectiva. (130-31)

Herein lies the key to Marqués' play, for it is the creation of a particular "angle of perspective" that governs both form and content in this play and that communicates the final message.

The play develops around the political situation on a small island obviously meant to be Puerto Rico. The seemingly powerful governor, Don José, is in reality plagued by a spiritual weakness epitomized by the fact that he has betrayed his original ideals of "pan, tierra, emancipación" in exchange for personal power. To disguise his weakness, he convinces himself and his followers that promoting the island's dependence on the affluent North is the only answer to the problems facing his country. A series of confrontations between Don José and the other major characters together with the interspersing of the statements of Don José's ideological rival, Don Rodrigo, serve to present the opposing side of the issue: that the Island's economic and political dependence on the North is a betrayal of its cultural essence, the heart of its existence. The play, however, becomes more complex than what critic Donald Shaw calls "straight social or political protest" ("*La muerte no entrará en palacio*: An Analysis" 31) because of the development of character in Don José's daughter Casandra. Her move from complete innocence to full awareness of the consequences of her father's actions parallels the political developments of the Island as it moves from the status of colony to that of protectorate. In the end,

Casandra embodies the warnings of the other characters who confront her father, as she becomes the dramatic agent that brings an end to Don José's life and to his treason. At the same time she raises her own sacrificial actions to the level of the heroic.

The play's virtual time and space (i.e., those which exist only as the play itself exists) operate on a dual level: one we might call universal, mythic or synchronic; and the other, present-day, re-interpreted reality, or diachronic. Through an expressionistic use of space, enhanced by creative use of light and sound, the play creates a tension between the synchronic and diachronic realms, in which the two alternately approach and distance one another. Only at the play's end do the two worlds fuse as God's judgment against the diachronic elements that would destroy the moral order of the universe is realized. This final impact carries a dual-level message: on the universal level, it says that truth and authenticity shall prevail; and on the regional level, it tells us that the specific mistakes of Muñoz Marín and those who followed him are redeemable through sacrificial and heroic actions.

The use of two characters borrowed from the classical theatrical tradition, Teresias and Casandra, and one myth-like character, Don Rodrigo, who in fact is based on the real, historical figure, Puerto Rican nationalist leader, Pedro Albizu Campos, creates the perspective in which the audience views the play's events. Through the dualities evident in each character the audience sees that the decisions and actions of individuals affect not only the everyday level of life in a particular place, but the moral order as well, thus acquiring significance on a universal level.

The dual role of the character Teresias communicates the synchronic/diachronic relationships within the play. The Tiresias of the Greek tradition, while never a major character, is important for his role as a visionary whose predictions are sought after for their wisdom and accuracy. Marqués' Teresias is on one hand a facsimile of the Greek character endowed with the power to explain the future, thus endowing his theatrical existence with a mythical quality; on the other hand, he is the friend and counsel of the governor's wife, Doña Isabel, and an old friend of Don José himself from a time when the two men shared the ideology of the governor's present enemy, Don Rodrigo. In this latter role, Teresias participates on the play's anecdotal level.

Teresias' solitary appearance in the play's opening scene evokes the frame of myth which surrounds the reality-based world of the play—a frame which subsequently creates a microcosmic world within its larger universe. In the typical Marqués manner, the stage is at first empty, as a magnified voice which seems to come from everywhere at once prepares Teresias' arrival as well as his role on the level of myth. The voice says: "Así ves tú el cuadro, Teresias. Así lo ves" (190). Our attention is then focused upon the figure of a near-sighted old man, cleaning his glasses, whose attention, in turn, is focused on the audience. In his stage directions, Marqués says the following: "Y sus grandes ojos miopes, al abrirse totalmente, miran al modo que lo hacen los niños cuando descubren mundos que están más allá de la realidad circundante" (191). Immediately the play estab-lishes that we are about to see a vision of the future filtered to us through a most unlikely character.

Teresias, because of his association with his classical role as visionary, gains credibility in Marqués play. When, in the opening speech he says: "Así veo yo el cuadro. Así veo yo a Casandra. . . . No ha sucedido, pero sucederá" (191), the audience can accept his words with confidence since in his historical theatrical role, his predictions are always accurate. Furthermore, the mythical aspect of his character that Teresias portrays in the opening scene leads the audience to view the play's events not only as what might have been but also as what will be, on a symbolic level, in the future. Teresias, then, literally allows us to "see" the universal repercussions of the temporal choices which Don José has made, the significance of which most of the play's other characters do not wholly perceive.

Don José's and Teresias' confrontation in the first *cuadro* of Act Two illuminates for us this perspective in which we perceive the impossibility of any kind of synchronization between the universal and the temporal. Teresias says to Don José: "El tiempo de mi realidad está varios compases más adelante que el tiempo de la tuya. . . . Tu mundo y mi mundo no podrán jamás sincronizarse. . . ." (268). Here Teresias continues by emphasizing the difference in the way the two former friends view the present crisis facing their homeland and even acknowledges a desire on Don José's part to understand the opposing side of the issue. Later on, Teresias accuses the governor of betraying the former ideals in exchange for personal power. He says: "Tu nombre aparecerá en los textos escolares de la Historia. A donde no llegará nunca es al libro que escriben los dioses para la inmortalidad" (269). Thus, the visionary reminds us, the audience, of his own rela-tionship with the gods which we have already witnessed. At the same time, he firmly places Don José on the temporal plane of specific events from which he cannot rise because of his narrowness of understanding of the larger significance of his own actions.

The character Casandra also fulfills a dual role: on the one hand she is Don José's daughter, a naive young girl in love with Alberto, the son of another of Don José's former friends. On the other hand, she fulfills a mythical and symbolic role because of her relationship to the classical Cassandra. Our first contact with Casandra is in her role on the temporal, anecdotal level. As she moves from innocence to knowledge on this level she also moves closer and closer to her mythical role. The classical Greek Cassandra is, like the classical Tiresias, a visionary. Unlike him, her predictions are neither sought after nor believed. They are, however, always accurate, and in her traditional role she is a voice of doom. Throughout *La muerte no entrará en palacio,* Don José repeatedly disregards the warnings that the other characters give him. As Casandra's character develops from innocence to knowledge, she embodies all of these unheeded warnings and acts as their agent. In the final scene, the universal and the temporal fuse in her as she speaks as a "voice" and loses her identity as an individual.

The change in Casandra's level of awareness is evident between *cuadros* one and two of the first act. We first see her with her fiancé Alberto, as a frivolous and naive, but optimistic youth. She expresses her optimism to Alberto: "Todo está en orden en el mundo: hay un sol y un mar; hay una ceiba que nos protege del sol y unas murallas que nos protegen del mar. Hay un palacio y un pueblo. El amor entró en palacio y el pueblo es feliz. Todo está en orden en el mundo" (199). As Alberto responds to her optimism and lack of vision with "En *tu* mundo" he opens the door to her education. She attempts to justify her point of view by repeating words she believes to be her mother's: "Nadie en palacio tiene derecho a la felicidad si el pueblo no es feliz" (199). Alberto points out to her, however, that those are the words of Don Rodrigo, whom Casandra knows only as her father's enemy.

The second *cuadro* shows many changes in Casandra. Six months have passed, during which time Don Rodrigo has returned to the Island from prison. Don José, out of fear, has forbidden his family the freedom to move between the palace and other parts of the Island. In this scene, Casandra's physical confinement corresponds antithetically to her developing intellectual enlightenment. On the one hand, she feels herself a prisoner, but at the same time, she reveals a new knowledge of the world. Throughout the play, this movement towards an understanding of the universal level on the part of the daughter serves constantly to make the audience aware of the father's inability to see the relationship of the temporal to the universal.

In the final *cuadro* of the play, Casandra moves closer to her role on the universal level and finally fuses the two roles to become not merely the voice of doom as is her classical counterpart, but also the instrument of divine justice. This scene, which begins as does the opening one, with the *Gran Voz* and Teresias, heard in the darkness of the stage, carries us momentarily back to the original framing device. The universal level is immediately evident in Teresias' psalm-like response to the Voice which he then addresses in a plea to stop the vision: "Mi hambre era de justicia. Mi sed, de amor. Calma sólo mi sed, Señor, y aparta de nos Tu justicia" (287). The Voice's response prepares the way for Casandra's entry on the scene: "Sólo por mi justicia calmaréis vuestra sed de amor" (287). This exchange between the mythical side of Terresias' role and the universal force which controls his vision introduces the element of divine justice. The final scene between the two lovers brings Casandra one step closer to her entry onto the universal level, but because she has not quite arrived at that full understanding she accidentally shoots the man she loves as she tries to prevent him from assassinating her father. At this point, she is still the governor's daughter.

In the play's final scene the integration of the universal and the temporal in Casandra is complete as she comes face to face with her father for the first time in the play. She is, however, no longer just Casandra-daughter, but is rather Casandra-daughter-prophetic voice-distributor of justice. In the course of her education she has adopted Alberto's ideals which are in turn those of Don Rodrigo. Significantly, in this scene, the light is on only Don José, and Casandra becomes literally and figuratively a voice in the darkness. She accuses her father of the destruction of her world if he signs the Commonwealth agreement and gradually adds all past voices of doom to her own. Don José methodically avoids showing recognition of any complicity or guilt on his part as he responds to each of her accusations by blaming someone else, thus demonstrating a view of himself as victim of others rather than victimizer. In this self-portrayal, Don José makes the distance between himself and his temporal world and Casandra's broader viewpoint even greater and more unsurpassable.

In the final moment when she kills Don José, Casandra fully embodies both worlds, as her words reveal: "¡Esa voz es mi voz! ¡La voz de mi mundo arrasado por ti! La voz de tus ideales muertos, de nuestra patria entregada, de mi amor asesinado" (323). In her words, we note the personal affronts she has suffered, i.e. the destruction of her own protected and safe world; the ideological aspects in the form of her father's betrayal of his own ideals and of his homeland; and the sacrifice of her love as she becomes symbolically and actually the standard bearer for the lost ideals. All of these elements relating to the more specific events, combined symbolically within a myth-like voice, create the effect of fusion of the universal and specific realms.

The dual role of the character Don Rodrigo, who is Don José's enemy, embodies the crisis which motivates the play's development. This dramatically interesting character, who never appears on stage, seems more of a myth than either Teresias or Casandra, even though he is based on a totally historical personage. Within the play he is the complete opposite of Don José. This dichotomy seems true to the real-life personages, Pedro Albizu Campos and Luis Muñoz Marín. Maldonado Denis implies the synchronic/diachronic difference between the two as he eulogizes Albizu Campos in *Puerto Rico: Mito y Realidad:* "Albizu Campos . . . sería como el Cid, que ganaría sus batallas aún después de muerto" (186). Even here the myth-like quality in the Nationalist leader—whether inherent or created—is apparent and it is this same quality which gives being to Don Rodrigo in Marqués' play. His voice in the darkness, as well as the words he pronounces which are based on Biblical prophecies, endow him with the myth-like quality. Throughout the course of the play, his words form an allegory of the events taking place, emphasizing his relationship to Don José in which the invisible Don Rodrigo seems to be the conscience of his former follower.

Although Don Rodrigo's voice is heard only a few times in the play, the allegorical nature of his words imposes his universal presence on the individual level. He always speaks with a resonant, amplified voice, an effect which equates him in one way with the god-like voice that speaks to Teresias. Don Rodrigo gives a symbolic interpretation in retrospect and with foreshadowing as he imitates the voice of doom:

Y cayeron las lluvias, y los ríos salieron de madre, y soplaron los vientos y dieron con ímpetu sobre la casa, mas no fue destruida porque estaba fundada sobre piedra . . . Pero la casa no es ya de piedra! Porque los fariseos despreciaron la piedra nuestra y edificaron su ostentoso edificio sobre cimientos falsos. Por eso yo os digo: Cuando lleguen las lluvias, cuando se desborde el torrente de los ríos, cuando soplen los vientos y den con ímpetu sobre la casa, ¡la casa será derribada! (141-142)

At this point, Don José has already rejected as worthless a stone which a group of peasants, hoping to establish an indigenous foundation for their Island's economy, had brought to him. Don Rodrigo's words first present the Biblical parable, establishing credibility on a universal level, then they relate to the rejection of the stone, allegorically equating Don José's rejection of the peasants to the false foundations on which this governor is building the new Commonwealth. The prophetic words then carry us forward to the end of Don José's "kingdom" and the end of the play when death literally enters the palace as Casandra kills her father.

The presentation of the conflict between Don José and the other characters leads to a kind of syllogistic trick which forces the audience to see Don José's position as wrong. In the first *cuadro*, the governor rationally presents his position in a conversation with Doña Isabel: . . . "el sentimentalismo ha mantenido a nuestro pueblo en la más abyecta miseria. . . . Nuestra historia ha sido una pueril sucesión de estallidos emocionales que no han conducido a parte alguna. Era ya hora de que la razón dominara a la emoción. Nos ha tocado vivir en la hora del progreso. . . ." (211-212). Don José's position, taken out of context, appears to be a positive one: that the use of reason over emotions can combat the physical misery of the Island people; his way of achieving that goal is by encouraging economic aid from the North. This seemingly desirable position becomes an undesirable one, however, because of a difference in the definition of emancipation. Don José's concept of freedom is that of freedom from hunger, or economic security. Representatives of the other side of the issue see it differently. The *Mozo* expresses it for the people's delegation: "me parece que no gozamos de la libertad fundamental . . . de ser nosotros mismos" (222). This concept of freedom proves to be even more desirable because of the number of persons in favor of it; it is further reinforced by the physical representation of the palace as a prison. The trick of logic occurs in the basic conflict of ideals: that of dependence *on* or independence *from* the North. Don José is in favor of dependence; the others are against it. Therefore, he is their enemy. The others are in favor of spiritual freedom. Don José, their enemy, opposes spiritual freedom; thus, he is wrong. The element of protest develops out of the correlation which the audience makes between reality and fiction and the right and wrong of the issue as the play presents it. Since at the writing of the play in 1956, Puerto Rico was already a protectorate of the United States, the play's position regarding that agreement is clearly one of dissent.

In addition to being an instrument of protest, the play serves a dual educational function: first, as a warning that economic dependence on the more affluent political powers is a threat to the Island people's very cultural existence; and second, as a suggestion of the necessity for some kind of sacrificial action to redeem the errors of the past. The use of music and the extinguishing of light as cues in conjunction with the scenes, constitute the warning element of the play. Teresias' role as a prophet in the framing scenes, emphasizing Don José's lack of understanding, influences the audience's perception of these cues. As the play opens, the stage is in shadows; the only noises are the sound of the tree frog (the *coquí*) and music described as "difusa, vaga, irreal" (190). The music and tree frog continue, according to the stage directions, long enough to cause uneasiness in the audience until Teresias comes on stage and begins his monologue. Lighting and music remain unchanged throughout the speech and only give way to a more realistic setting after Teresias finishes. Through his words he indicates that he offers the play as an explanation. The lighting and music remind the audience of that fact in five major scenes, each of which reinforces a principal aspect of the issue. Each of these scenes takes place in shadows or complete darkness, often with only one character illuminated as the music plays in the background. The association between these particular effects with Teresias' visionary role serves to remove the audience's attention momentarily from the play's action and re-focus it on the framing scenes and on the element of warning, causing the viewers to think about the issue rather than what is happening to a particular character.

Casandra's change from ignorance of the farcical life which her father has created for her to recognition of the falseness of that world demonstrates the need for sacrificial action as a means of resolving the problem which the play presents. Her role adds a human dimension to the political issue, since the controversy affects her through her love for Alberto and her ties to her family. She plays the child who discovers not only that her father is a phony, but that her world is also false. Her growing consciousness gains the audience's sympathy as it underscores the action that results from awareness. Therefore, when Casandra takes the final step of killing her father, the audience can support that action. Her final portrayal in the form of a statue, is an indication of the immortality that goes with sacrificial action.

The dominance of the justice of God in the moral order of the world remains central to the play's development and resolution. By presenting contemporary events from a historical and mythical perspective, René Marqués lifts the play out of the political protest syndrome to a level which carries the play past the specific Puerto Rican circumstance. In the same way that Don José passes judgment on those whom he governs and whose destiny he tries to determine, the play itself passes judgment on and condemns Don José, whose short-sighted, individual actions would destroy the moral order of the universe.

Marqués' other historical play, _Mariana o el alba_ (1965), is based on an actual happening, _The Grito de Lares,_ which was a short-lived rebellion of 1868 against Spain's colonialism in Puerto Rico. The historical details of the play are faithfully researched and are presented in a setting which painstakenly recreates the luxurious _hacienda_ life of the period. The work, however, rises above its historical realism to become a challenge offered to the would-be heroes of the present who symbolically are made accomplices in the Puerto Rican fight for freedom. Because the patriotic meaning is embedded in historical fact and its criticism is not leveled at any one specific person, this play, a favorite of Puerto Rican audiences, is often presented and has not been subjected to censorship as has _La muerte no entrará en palacio._

A small group of wealthy landowners carried out the rebellion that has come to be called the _Grito de Lares._ These rebels, protesting the unfair taxes levied by Spain as well as the authoritarianism to which they were subjected, were followers of don Ramón Emeterio Betances. The well-known patriot was living in exile in Santo Domingo (in 1868 an independent nation) where he was attempting to gather support of arms, men and money for the independence movement in Puerto Rico. At that time, patriots such as Betances from all three Spanish-speaking islands (Cuba, Santo Domingo and Puerto Rico) supported the ideal of a Federation of the Spanish-speaking Antilles. The small group of Betances' followers waited in vain for word from him and for the much-needed aid he was supposedly sending them. As news of the imminent rebellion reached the Spanish military, however, the Puerto Ricans could wait no longer, and so on the evening of September 23, 1868, they overpowered a small force of Spanish soldiers in Lares, raised the flag made and partially designed by Mariana Bracetti, thus proclaiming the Republic of Puerto Rico, abolishing slavery and the hated system of identification cards which all Puerto Ricans were required to carry. The rebellion was revealed to the Spaniards, possibly by someone from among the rebels themselves, and the Republic lasted only twenty-four hours.

The play's historical accuracy, so important to its development, was a difficult achievement since at the time of the play's writing, there existed very little published information on the details of the rebellion. Marqués, in his dedicatory statement to the play, credits his long-time friend, José Lacomba, for these details: "Al profesor José Manuel Lacomba, sin cuya tesonera búsqueda de datos históricos y generoso estímulo, esta obra probablemente jamás se habría escrito" (Centennial Edition 7). In an unpublished paper on *Mariana o el alba*, Lacomba recalls his search for the historical facts: "I handled the information bit by bit as I found it in libraries and in interviews with people who could remember some historical detail about the revolution of Lares and about the figure of Mariana" (4). To demonstrate Marques' faithfulness to those facts, Lacomba recounts how the play originally ended with the birth of Mariana's son who symbolized "the fight for the independence of the Island initiated by men and women of the last century" (5). While doing some later research, however, he discovered that Mariana had had a miscarriage while imprisoned. Marqués then changed the play's ending, having Mariana deliver a stillborn child in a makeshift Spanish prison; and in this way, he transformed the play from a substantially straightforward patriotic work into a challenge to the would-be heroes of the present.

Mariana o el alba's realistic, historical perspective, presented with an overlay of double meanings and symbolism, instills the play with a greater significance arising from the relationship between the past and the present. Always in the background is the present fact that of the three Spanish-speaking Caribbean islands, Puerto Rico is the only one not an independent nation, and thus does not have a clear "identidad propia." While the work does not level criticism directly at any specific persons or events (as does *La muerte no entrará en palacio*), it *does* raise the 1868 rebellion to a heroic level, making of it an unfulfilled revolution, just as the protagonist, Mariana, is an unfulfilled mother when she delivers a stillborn child at the end of the play.

Both revolution and mother wait for another child to complete that which has been started.

J. L. Styan, in *Drama, Stage and Audience*, perceptively discusses a concept which he calls "emergent meaning" in relationship to a play's development—a concept which illuminates for us the unfolding of Marqués' play. In this concept, Styan compares a play to a poem. The poem, he says, has an inherent quality, so that even a dissected poem still "remains itself." He sees the play as "a growing organism, reborn at each performance" whose meaning "is in the growth and not the unrealized intention" (27). He continues by saying that "the power and depth of the play's emergent meaning is directly related to its rhythm and form. In its own temporal and spatial dimensions, tempo and shape control the intensity with which an audience receives its image" (28). And, "Form is not a pattern for conformity; it is created to satisfy the organic needs of an audience in their response to the play" (29). In this play by René Marqués, a system of dualities forms the work's basic structure. The meaning "emerges," in the sense in which Styan uses the term, as the play develops from what would seem at first to be a straightforward, historical account of a patriotic event into the revolutionary challenge it becomes, in which are united past and present. The play's historical realism, rooted in an actual happening and a specific situation develops within a politico-economic environment in which the spectator recognizes a close resemblance to that of the present age. The dual role of the protagonist, Mariana Bracetti, who is wife, expectant mother, homemaker, as well as a revolutionary heroine whose personal goals and desires give way to patriotic obligations and sacrifices, is the key to the spectator's perception of the play's ultimate message. Finally, the play's dual characteristics merge in Mariana's child who is at once a representative of the personal and of the patriotic hopes for the future; and only in his stillbirth (reminiscent of today's "status quo") does the play's true identity as a voice for the unfulfilled independence become clear.

The well-known supporter of Puerto Rican independence, Manuel Maldonaldo Denis comments on the relationship between the actual *Grito de Lares* and the present independence movement:

> La vigencia del Grito de Lares como acontecimiento histórico debe entenderse a la luz de la vigencia de la independencia como única solución anti-imperialista al problema colonial de Puerto Rico. Si muriese el movimiento independentista moriría también el Grito de

Lares en la conciencia colectiva de nuestro pueblo." (*Puerto Rico: Mito y Realidad* 252)

Clearly, there does exist a public for whom the play's topic is meaningful in itself. However, the relationship which develops between past and present is the message carrier in this work.

The total interdependence of past and present carries the patriotic experience of the characters into the world of the spectator. José Lacomba acknowledges this relationship when he notes that in *Mariana o alba* "history is of actual presence, a vicarious experience" (11). Tamara Holzapfel also refers to the unique existence of past and present. She says: "The author's endeavor to recreate the flavor of a bygone era is evident on every page. His effort to commemorate the past as well as to inspire present-day Puerto Ricans with a patriotic message is eminently successful" ("In Search of Identity and Form" 162). The goals of the play's characters continually reach into the future. The future, however, for those patriots, is the present of the spectator. Susanne Langer views the virtual future created in a play as "destiny." She explains:

> Destiny is, of course, always a virtual phenomenon—there is no such thing in cold fact. It is a pure semblance. But what it "resembles" ... is nonetheless an aspect of real experience, and, indeed, a fundamental one, which distinguishes human life from animal existence: the sense of past and future as parts of one continuum, and therefore of life as a single reality." (*Feeling and Form* 311)

This latter idea is the basis for the time relationship in Marqués' play, thus establishing a direct link between the heroes of the past to those possible ones of the future/present—for as long as they sit in the theatre house viewing the play, at any rate.

The play's dual identity gradually develops in three stages which correspond respectively to the three acts and are centered around the protagonist, Mariana. This heroine's dual identity, reflected in the work's title, in her own daily life, and in the political environment is the key that opens the door to our perception of the emergent meaning. The first act serves as an introduction to the specific situation in which the characters must act and lays the foundation for the transference of past to present. Act two establishes the symbolic correspondence between the developing rebellion and the child which the protagonist is expecting. The final act whose scenario is Mariana's prison, completes ironically the correspondence, as the child whose conception and growth has paralleled the developing fight for freedom is born dead.

The play's title reflects the duality of the individual vs. the collective society, as well as the making of a choice. The use of the protagonist's first name, "Mariana," personalizes our perception of the heroine's actions. The historical Mariana was Mariana Bracetti de Rojas and she was known to sign her letters and other communiqués as "Brazo de Oro" (editor's note to the Centennial Edition 10). In the play, however, the family name is not emphasized and the revolutionary name is never mentioned. To have done so would have destroyed the tension between the personal and the heroic qualities. The word "alba" (dawn) of the title has a double meaning in most all languages: one, it refers to that specific time of a day when the sun is rising; and two, it often implies the future or a new beginning. As we will see at the end of the play, it simultaneously conveys both meanings to the viewer. Also significant is the adoption of the word "o" (or), rather than "and," for instance. This word implies that there must be a choice: the individual, or the future of the society. In the heroic (as this work portrays it) there cannot be both.

Mariana's daily life and activities further substantiate the duality reflected in the work's title. She is at once a nearly perfect "ama de casa," or housewife, and a person whose very liberal ideas are not appropriate for a "perfect" housewife of the past century. The fact that Mariana is on stage when the curtain first opens on this play is significant to the development of her dual role. This is perhaps the only dramatic work of Marqués which does not open onto an empty stage. In this play, the author gives several pages of minuscule details of setting—even colors of pillows, etc.—to recreate faithfully the elegance of the wealthy *hacienda* life. Mariana appears to us as an integral part of this luxurious setting, leaving no doubt as to her background and, because of her liberal ideas, establishing more firmly the duality. We first see her in her "feminine" role, putting the finishing touches on a dress she has made for her goddaughter Rosaura. Thus, our first visual impression of the protagonist is that of a wealthy, elegant "lady" both in her surroundings and her activities.

Her liberal ideas become apparent immediately, however, in her conversation with Nana Monse, the black, former slave who raised Mariana from a child. The spectator learns that as a child the protagonist was introduced to the works of Diderot, Rousseau and Voltaire, all synonomous with liberalism. Her attitude towards slavery and racial integration makes explicit her position on this issue. She allows and even encourages an intimate relationship between her goddaughter and Nana Monse's son, Redención, whose freedom Mariana's father bought at the boy's baptism. She goes on to define freedom as she says to Nana Monse: "La libertad no es dolor, ni separación. Es amor. Es unión. Unión de todos los seres humanos en un mismo plano de dignidad, igualdad, fraternidad. . . ." (34). The protagonist's definition is broad enough to encompass both levels of the play—the individual and the society, thus making it meaningful across time barriers rather than specifically related to this one particular historical event.

The protagonist's ideals of freedom are further reflected in her position in the specific political environment as we see her not only as the wife of one of the leaders of the rebellion, but also as a respected equal among the revolutionaries. Contrasting to a scene in which Mariana, the seamstress, fits the dress on Rosaura, is the following one in which she clearly reveals her revolutionary role. A peasant named Manolo comes to tell her husband, Miguel, that they must pay more money for arms they are purchasing. Mariana not only handles the problem but gives the money to the peasant for the purchase. These decisive political actions, while not in contrast to the protagonist's own personality, do contrast directly to her more feminine role of 19th- century lady.

The first act serves not merely to introduce the play's dualities, but to build the actual foundation for the past-present relationship of those dualities. The development of this act reveals the existence of façade and reality in the lives of the characters, as well as in the life of the play's meaning. The façade-reality dichotomy is most clearly evident in two contrasting scenes: one, a dinner scene in which the revolutionaries serve as hosts to a number of people who represent "the other side," including the top ranking Spanish Official for the Lares region; and, two, the act's final scene in which the rebels pledge their dedication to the cause for which they are fighting. The author's stage directions, which introduce the dinner scene, serve as an example of the dual nature of this scene:

> En las escenas que se inician, precediendo a la cena, y después de ésta (en el Cuadro II) debe tenerse en cuenta que el drama soterrado entre puertorriqueños y criollos de un lado y españoles y españolizantes de

> otro estará, de parte de los personajes más cultos, envuelto en la exquisitez del trato social, en una época cuando la conversación no era mero hablar para la comunicación directa, sino un arte cultivado hasta el refinamiento. Así, frases aceradas o irónicas se dicen con la más encantadora de las sonrisas, lo ofensivo de algunas insinuaciones o frases ambiguas no sólo se disimula bajo la forma ingeniosa de decirlas, sino bajo el gesto cortés y galante. . . . (60)

In this scene, the spectator has no choice except to view negatively the Spaniards and their sympathizers because of their failure to comprehend fully the overlay of courtesy which disguises the true feelings of the Puerto Ricans.

In contrast, after the last guest has left and the revolutionaries are re-united in Mariana's living room, all façade disappears and the scene, whose impact is replete with irony, takes on the appearance of a ceremonial promise of patriotic loyalty. The stage directions once again reveal the nature of this scene: "La actitud de los personajes ahora es distinta. Prescinden de cortesías, ambages y circunloquios. Hombres y mujeres se tratan como compañeros de lucha, actitud por completo ajena a la prevaleciente en la reunión social anterior" (114). This episode projects the revolutionaries' seriousness, in comparison to the frivolity and deceits of the previous scene.

A more symbolic aspect of the façade-reality dichotomy is evident in the final scene in which the characters enter into a theoretical and philosophical discussion of the flag they will wave and its symbolic meaning for them. In a final gesture of solidarity they each vow in a clasp of hands to live for the flag, to respect it, to love it, to fight for it, to kill for it, and to die for it (123). One cannot overlook the irony-filled impact of this scene. The heroic patriots' solemn vow, seen as totally dedicated in view of the contrasts prevalent here, is null and void in the present. In the Appendix to the play's Centennial Edition of the *Grito de Lares*, René Marqués poses the following questions:

> ¿Por qué a la Bandera de Lares (la más históricamente significativa, la que tiene prioridad revolucionaria en nuestra historia del pueblo), no se le da oficialmente e incluso extraoficialmente el crédito que merece en Puerto Rico? ¿Por qué ni siquiera a una de las varias facciones patrióticas puertorriqueñas se le ha ocurrido nunca adoptarla como emblema o insignia de la organización? ¿Qué pasa con nuestra conciencia histórica? ("La bandera de Lares" in the Appendix 243)

Thus, the emphasis and solemnity accorded the flag scene is of extreme importance to the developing meaning, as the audience of the present is forced to confront its lack of identity (in Marqués' opinion) through the association made between the flag of Lares and freedom, and through the basis of façade and underlying reality. This latter plants the suggestion that there is meaning for the present to be perceived beneath the historical surface.

The second act establishes the association between the unborn child and the pending revolution, as personal hopes and desires seem repeatedly to be truncated by loyalty and responsibilities to the group. This termination of the personal can be seen both in the juxtaposition of scenes as well as in the plot line itself. Two opening scenes serve as an example of the former. In typical Marqués fashion, this act begins with an empty stage. The offstage voices of Mariana and Nana Monse reveal that Mariana is expecting a child and the scene ends with Nana singing a lullaby. The onstage action which immediately follows, however, begins with another song—the present Puerto Rican state song "La Borinqueña," which Rosaura sings from offstage, using the 19th-century revolutionary words of the exiled poetess Lola Rodríguez de Tió ("La bandera de Lares" 242). In a like manner, Mariana no sooner tells her husband of the news of the expected child than they are interrupted by Miguel's brother Manuel who tells them the revolution must begin at once. In both cases the theatrical language of scene juxtaposition implies subordination of personal feelings to revolutionary obligations.

One by one, those things which have suggested hope for the future of a free Puerto Rico are destroyed, leaving, at the end, only the unborn child. The revolution fails, Redención is killed, symbolizing the death of racial freedom, as his dying brings an end to the possibility of his union with Rosaura. Miguel is in hiding and finally, Mariana is imprisoned. The child is mentioned twice, both times at moments when the tension reaches a point of exaltation: Miguel makes the association as he leaves for the attack saying: "Nuestro hijo nacerá en una patria libre" (156); and, Mariana repeats the phrase when she receives the mistaken news that the rebels have won. She speaks to the unborn child: "Nacerás libre. ¡Libre! . . . ¡Libre!" (175). Here the historical facts that Puerto Rico is not free and that the rebellion failed, contribute to the spectator's developing understanding of the play's meaning. However, despite one's knowledge of history, the child, as a source of hope, still offers a positive resolution for the play since there yet remains the expectation of his birth.

The correspondence between the child and the failed revolution is complete in the third act, and only then does the play's full meaning emerge. The change of location, the child's stillbirth, and the ironic freeing of the protagonist at the dawn, build on the previously established relationship between past and present to tell the audience that while the specific dawn of the heroes of the past is gone, the symbolic dawn of the future has arrived.

This act takes place on a split stage which depicts Mariana's very real prison and symbolizes her loss of even the personal freedom she has had up to this point. A large door of *ausubo* with an iron lock, a window with iron bars and the presence of a guard on the outside emphasize the fact that the protagonist is now a prisoner. In addition, a favorite recourse of Marqués, the use of a painted gauze curtain to form the fourth wall of the cell, makes Mariana's imprisonment total. The author describes the curtain as follows:

> "La cuarta pared de la celda, es decir, a la pared que se supone sea frontal . . . consiste de una gasa, pintada en su exterior imitando el mismo color y condición exterior del resto de la estructura. Esta gasa al iluminarse de frente, presentará aspecto de pared sólida. Pero al iluminarse la celda por dentro para la acción dramática que allí ocurra, la gasa se hará transparente, permitiendo la visión completa del interior." (213-214)

When the action takes place on the outside, this "wall" excludes Mariana from the scene, making evident her encarceration; and when the activity is on the inside, the locked door and window and the guard cause the same effect. Because we, as spectators, have associated her only with the luxurious surroundings in which the first part of the work occurs, and because she has come to signify the revolution, we are now able to appreciate the personal frustration and bitter disappointment of the play's heroes. This, combined with our perception of the work from our place in its future, makes us aware of the loss which exists in our present world.

The birth of the child is dramatically associated with imprisonment, death, and the failed revolution. Mariana responds to Nana's news that Miguel has been captured and may possibly suffer imprisonment or perhaps exile. She says: "¡La cárcel sólo; el destierro, quizás! ¿Pero no comprendes que esas son dos formas horribles de muerte también? ¿Miguel preso? ¡No! Mejor muerto. (Se aprieta el vientre con ambas manos en gesto de dolor. Su cuerpo dobla.) ¡Nana! ¡Ay,

Nana!" (229). The stage is then darkened, and when the transition is made to the next scene, the child has been born. The birth, seen against the background of the protagonist's own jail cell, becomes an integral part of her expressed feelings over her husband's imprisonment. If the father is better dead than in prison, why not the child?

The protagonist's decision to take the stillborn child with her when she is freed at dawn rather than to permit Nana to carry him away earlier creates the final step which will make the audience's understanding complete. The new mother insists: "¡No! No te lo llevarás. . . . Nació aquí conmigo, en las sombras. Y conmigo saldrá a enfrentarse al sol de este amanecer" (232). The dawn to which she refers here is the specific one of her present, and our past. With the child's death, the specific rebellion of 1868 at Lares comes to an end. The significance for the future—or, for the spectator, the present— only emerges, however, with the death. As Mariana finally leaves her cell, her words symbolically implicate the individuals of the present time in the unfulfilled revolution as she says to the Spanish Official: "Sin embargo, nacerán otros hijos, señor. Nacerán también en las sombras que ustedes han creado para ellos. Pero esos hijos, o los hijos de esos hijos, conocerán finalmente, sin temor, ¡a plenitud!, el sol radiante de la libertad" (238). The background music of "La Borinqueña" indicates the symbolic and the political nature of her statement. At the same time, the dead son she carries in her arms represents the personal sacrifices the heroes of the past made for those of the future. The spectators in the Puerto Rican audience, for whom this play is most meaningful, are the "other sons." Therefore, it is implicitly their duty to continue the fight for liberty and equality.

As this play develops toward its final resolution, the spectator becomes aware that the drama's fulfillment is unfulfillment, both of Mariana's specific motherhood and of the revolution's quest for liberty. In this unfulfillment, the individual's desires and hopes are sacrificed to lend hope to the future. Were Mariana's child to have lived, signifying the continuance of the revolution, the play would have a totally different meaning. As it is, the responsibility for the revolution against oppression is laid at the foot of all future generations, including that of the present one.

Each of these plays is based on historical facts: the signing of the commonwealth agreement by Governor Luis Muñoz Marín in 1952 and the ill-fated independence action of 1868 known as the *Grito de Lares*. In both cases, the dramatic relationship between the factual history and the play's resolutions create the relevance of history to the spectator's present. *La muerte no entrará en palacio* becomes a work of protest because of its creation after the commonwealth agreement had already been signed. At the same time, it is a suggestion of the heroic possibilities for those who oppose the dependence on the United States. One might even go so far as to project an accusation against those who did not act as does *Casandra* and are therefore responsible for the present-day situation. The same kind of relationship between historical fact and dramatic fiction transforms *Mariana o el alba* into a work that challenges the spectator of the present to fulfill the role of heroic freedom fighter. In each case, the work is brought to an end by a death that projects future actions into the realm of the viewers. Thus, the fulfillment of the plays' resolutions is the unfulfillment of the historical purposes.

Chapter VI

Entrapment and the Future

René Marqués' characters are always held accountable for their own actions, whose results are very seldom positive ones. Often his characters play out their drama within a limited space representing their living quarters, and from which they may not or will not leave. In *El apartamiento* and *La casa sin reloj*, the characters are trapped in these spaces because of their own fear of exposing themselves to the unknown. In each case, the result of this dependence on fear is either the fragmentation, but coexistence of past, present, and future within the space that the characters inhabit as in *El apartamiento*, or the suppression of time, which in the end cannot be ignored, as in *La casa sin reloj*. The resolution of each play points toward possible future directions for the characters. In turn, these possibilities serve as warning messages for the spectator.

When *El apartamiento* first appeared on stage (April 16, 1964) during the Seventh Annual Festival of Puerto Rican Theatre, critics received it ambiguously, lauding it for its fresh approach on the Puerto Rican stage and down-grading it because of a difficulty in understanding what it was really about. Angelina Morfi lauds the harmonious correspondence between form and content saying "Es por esa armonía entre fondo y forma que René Marqués logra en *El apartamiento* que la imagen desintegrada del hombre contemporáneo que nos muestra se pueda apreciar en toda la magnitud que requiere el problema" ("El Apartamiento: Nueva ruta" 27). On the other hand, upon the occasion of the play's premiere Antonio Pasarell wrote: "Es absurdo que estos seres humanos no tengan vida interior aún en medio del aislamiento. A mi juicio, nunca fueron artistas ni tuvieran imaginación ni voluntad" (" 'El Apartamiento': Impresiones" 27). The author's adaptation of techniques at that time associated with the European "theatre of the absurd" was responsible for creating a stumbling block to a complete understanding of the work on the part of some critics.

The play has been superficially linked to the theatre of the absurd and we can easily see how this correspondence was conceived. The work develops in an interior space, basically concerning two characters. The two protagonists carry out seemingly meaningless tasks and suffer from an apparent lack of communication as they would appear to portray the lack of escape from the anguish of the human condition. William Siemens discusses the play on the basis of what he calls a "schizoid psychic state." He concludes that "The value of the play among its contemporaries lies, perhaps, in its vision—an accurate one—of modern America exhibiting schizoid characteristics on account of her choice of security over identity and stimulation" ("Assault on the Schizoid Wasteland" 23). While Siemens states accurately the play's protest of the choice of security over identity and stimulation, his view of this work touches only superficially and in a contrived way, the play's message, but not its emergent meaning, in the sense in which J. L. Styan uses the term. Daniel Zalacaín acknowledges that Marqués is not a writer of "theatre of the absurd" in the European sense of Ionesco or Beckett and goes on to call Marqués' works in which he adapts techniques of the theatre of the absurd, *absurdist*. Zalacaín bases his opinion on the author's commitment to the Puerto Rican social reality which prevents Marqués from following the "philosophy of *derrota* of the dramatists of the absurd ("René Marqués, del absurdo a la realidad" 35). This view, too, is incomplete, however, for it fails to take into account the meaning which develops from the experience of the play itself. He concludes: "Es en el pasado donde se encuentra la raíz de lo autóctono y lo auténtico, integrantes fundamentales de su identidad. Y como figura simbólica de la visión redentora del alma, el autor presenta al indio. A través del indio, René Marqués trata de buscar la identidad del puertorriqueño con el resto de Iberoamérica" (35). Again, this conclusion, stated in thematic terms only, does not even acknowledge the experience either of the characters or of the audience.

Three years after the premiere of *El apartamiento, Asomante* published an article by Marqués which he had written about the theatre of Luigi Pirandello. Today, what Marqués had to say about the famous Italian playwright illuminates for us both the ultimate meaning and the style of *El apartamiento*. Of Pirandello he says: "El problema que plantea dramáticamente Pirandello con enfoque moderno (aunque sus raíces se remonten a los presocráticos) es, dentro de su aparente sencillez, de profundidad estremecedora. La unicidad o multiplicidad de la existencia" (Marqués on Pirandello 33). Similarly, one can say of Marqués in *El apartamiento* that he too plants dramatically the problem of the multiplicity of existence. Indeed, all elements of this play, within its own temporal and spatial configurations point to this "multiplicity of existence," not only with a "modern" focus, but with a Spanish American one as well.

Marqués elaborates on this idea by referring to what he calls the power of thinking. He states that thought cannot in the end give the only true reality—the objective one—but rather, it gives multiple images creating a multiplicity of supposed realities. According to Marqués, "El pensamiento no es sólo un espejo recto o liso que en última instancia pudiera reflejar 'científicamente' la realidad objetiva, sino simultáneamente, espejo cóncavo y convexo, que multiplica, distorsiona y deforma aquella imagen verdadera que objetivamente intentábamos descubrir, y la cual, por lo tanto, será siempre inasible para nosotros" (Marqués on Pirandello 33). Seen in this light, Marqués' play is a dramatization of the multiple realities created by the thought or the innermost consciousness of the co-protagonists. As the play develops, the characters alternately affirm and deny their various "realities" as they travel deeper and deeper into their subconscious to the point of affirming a collective, but Spanish American, historical consciousness, of which both characters seem to have been unaware. In the final analysis, the play's resolution is left open, thus forcing the emergent meaning to be related to the spectator's futile search for objectivity in the characters' identities.

In his discussion of communication in drama, J. L. Styan emphasizes the importance of the spectator in any critical analysis of a dramatic work. According to Styan: "The inference from example after example is that in the theatre experience it is not so much the elements of drama on the stage or the perceptions of the audience which are important, as the relationships between them. In the mesh of every successful performance, the signals from the script to the actor, and from the actor to the spectator and back again, complete a dramatic circuit of which the audience is an indispensable part" (*Drama, Stage and Audience* 24). In building on this communicative relationship between the work and the spectator, Styan proposes his concept of "emergent meaning." In Styan's view, the meaning of any dramatic work is in the experience itself, or in other words, the growth of the play from beginning to end, at which point the full meaning "emerges" (27). Herein lies the key to a more complete perception of

Marqués' play, which, to be understood, must be considered holisti-
cally.   An examination of the relationship between the work in
production and the spectator underscores the fact that the completed
play itself is the message, while the meaning behind the message is
based on the spectator's viewing experience.

The play takes place in a self-contained, futuristic style apartment from which the two protagonists may not, and indeed have no
physical need, to leave. Food arrives already prepared by means of a
dumbwaiter, dishes are disposible, and the laundry arrives clean and
pressed.   This is the ultimate in convenience living, making the
familiar electric appliances of the spectator's contemporary world
obsolete things of the past. Although there is a suggestion of some
police-type authority who physically confines the protagonists to
their apartment/prison (Isabel Cuchi Coll S-4, S-18 and Francisco
Arriví 10), René Marqués contends that "en cuanto a lo de policíaco, en
pirmer [sic] lugar, lo es, en sentido de que hay un misterio por resolver
pero, no hay policías, ni detectives, porque el crimen a que se refiere
esta *encerrona* no es de la incumbencia de las autoridades policíacas"
(Marqués in Cuchi Coll interview). He goes on to ay that the "enclosure" is, rather, the concern of "la Humanidad toda, o más
específicamente a aquella parte de la Humanidad que comprende la
super-civilizada cultura occidental" (S-18). The basic conflict which
causes the protagonists' anguish is not simply "the human condition"
per se, but rather that of the Iberoamerican individual who struggles
for a satisfying identity between his "super-civilized" occidental culture and his Spanish American one, made unique in his work by the
Indian presence.

The main characters, Carola and Elpidio, spend their time at
seemingly meaningless, but highly specialized, tasks. She measures
an endless blue ribbon and he unsuccessfully attempts to put together
a jigsaw puzzle of a human figure. Dialogue between these two and
later between them and the other characters takes place while they
attend to their tasks, although they do leave their places or become
distracted occasionally. The colorless, sterile stage set reinforces the
futility of their efforts, as does a large door that supposedly serves no
functional purpose since there is no exit from the apartment building
to the outside. The protagonists use the door frequently, however, as
they take turns searching for an exit. Furthermore, the doorbell
repeatedly interrupts their work to announce a series of unexpected
and unexplained arrivals which initiate action and create tension:

first, useless electric appliances, then, at intervals, the other characters of the play.

The first characters to arrive are Terra and Lucío, who represent both the main characters' youth as well as their creative abilities (Carola it appears was a poetess, and Elpidio, a musician). Another pair, Cuprila and Landrilo, who arrive in the second act, are the inspectors whose duty it is to see that no rules are broken by those assigned to the apartment (rules which include no visitors and no memories of the past). Together, these two sets of pairs personify the play's inner tension: that of the desire to acknowledge or to find one's own unique identity vs. the fear of the unknown results in doing so. The final arrival is a single character, the Iberoamerican Indian, Tlo, who not only interrupts the symmetry of the pairs but also the starkness of the set with his colorful Indian dress. The co-protagonists vacilate repeatedly between an alliance with their creative potential, as Terra and Lucío represent it, and their fear, in the form of obediance to the two inspectors who finally order them to kill the Indian. This mandate forces Carola and Elpidio into the only really decisive action which either of them carry out and Carola chooses to free the Indian rather than to kill him. The play comes to an end as the doorbell rings again and the characters affirm its ambiguity. For Elpidio it may be the return of the inspectors and death, and for Carola, the return of the Indian and freedom. Here the spectator is left to formulate his/her own opinion since the curtain falls before Carola opens the door.

In *El apartamiento*, the space and time configurations are the key to the relationship between the work and the spectator in which the latter's experience of the play is analogous to that of the characters' experience of the events of the play. As multiple meanings and parallels constantly complement and contradict one another, seem to correspond symmetrically, yet do not, the play vacilates between negations and affirmations of its own reality, as well as that of the characters. The work becomes like a mirror of mankind as he/she plays out multiple roles in an interiorized, timeless space. This playing out of roles is unified by a certain progression in the questioning of self until the characters literally and symbolically free their collective historical consciousness, which the Indian character personifies.

The way in which Marqués uses time and space creates a stark, confined interior atmosphere in which his characters play out the many roles which live in their innermost thoughts and contribute to their own identity. The development of the work for the characters can be seen, as Victoria Espinosa has stated, as "la confrontación misma de la personalidad" ("El Apartamiento" 34). There is much more to the work than this, however, since the spectator, as he/she experiences the constant shifting back and forth and the tension between fear of the unknown and the desire for the freedom of individuality, finds him/herself on his/her own personal quest as he/she searches for the "reality" portrayed. Tension between a false linear progression and a temporal relationship among the characters in which all times seem to co-exist, plus the fact that the play's resolution is left open forces the emergent meaning to be related to the spectator's futile search for objectivity in the characters' identities. The viewer must ask "Who is real?", "What is true?", "Who is responsible?", and "Is there any way out?"

Several referents of time point to concepts of "progress" in the sense of linear movement or at the very least, change, from one time unit to another. One of the most obvious is the underlying "suspense" story. The two characters break the rules they are obligated to keep if they are to remain in the "security" of their living quarters. Their insurrections progress from simply bringing in mysterious and use- less gifts which appear outside of the door to allowing Terra and Lucío to lure them to memories of their past creative selves. We wait then for something to happen to them for their insubordination. But, even with the arrival of the inspectors with all their threats, nothing ever really *happens* to Carola and Elpidio.

The various arrivals also denote a certain linear movement. The first arrival is a small electric iron, the next, a large dishwasher. These appliances are then followed by the appearance of Terra and Lucío, followed by the inspectors, Cuprila and Landrilo and finally, Tlo. While there does appear to be a linear progression here, the various arrivals are actually unrelated to each other on any time line. They are, however, related to the protagonists' questioning of their own existence in the apartment as the focal point of their doubts moves from the physical outer world to the inner psychological one.

The tasks themselves would seem to be time-related since first of all, these charactes spend most of their time at their specialized jobs. The very act of measuring indicates a beginning and end. Carola's ribbon, though, is endless. It comes from one basket to go into an identical one on the othe side of the table and her counting never ends, even when she arrives at zero (she is counting backwards), at which point she continues with negative numbers. Elpidio's task, too, is of a sort that should have a definitive end, for puzzles exist to be assembled; but he is never able to make all the pieces fit, so that job, like Carola's, is an endless one.

The characters are also time markers. Carola and Elpidio mark the present by virtue of being protagonists. Moreover, the on-going nature of the tasks they perform, in combination with the "eternal present" of the theatre, indicates these two characters' "presentness." Lucío and Terra represent the past obviously by the stories they tell of their former associations with the protagonists. In addition, a blue light which always marks their presence and is associated with a dreamlike state, reminds the spectator that these two characters do in fact represent a different era than that of the present. Cuprila and Landrilo, while guardians of the "present" apartment, also stand for the future since it is in their power to control the destiny of Carola and Elpidio as long as the latter remain subservient. The appearance of the Indian Tlo adds an element of the historical since he does not belong to the immediate past of either character, but rather to a remote, even forgotten past, belonging to them as Spanish Americans.

Despite the apparent progress which the characters and spectator notice in the various arrivals, the time relationships which the spectator notes among the characters serve to undo the more secure feeling of linear progression. The viewer has no way of knowing which, of things and people, if any, were already present at the beginning of the play and which will return again. There is certainly no doubt that at the play's end, the unanswered doorbell could signal the arrival of either the inspectors or of Tlo. There is no way of knowing which it is. The spectator can only conjecture an answer. Some viewers might even contemplate the arrival of yet another, heretofore unknown, facet of the characters' realities.

All of this, together with the textual suggestions that all arrivals are connected to Carola and Elpidio's innermost thoughts guide the spectator to respond by evaluating the multiple facets of the co-protagonists' personalities. Carola's and Elpidio's complex of distinguishing characteristics are antagonistic forces which seem to co-exist in a pattern of alternating dominance: the creative potential, once developed but later abandoned and forgotten; the fear of losing a convenient life whose details are attended to by some invisible and unknown power; and semi-consciousness of a remote past never totally perceived but always in the background.

The enclosed, limited space becomes the factor which helps the spectator find the possibility of meaning at the play's end. The enclosure itself has a double meaning. According to Marqués: "*Apartamiento* es regionalismo puertorriqueño . . . para departamento. El título tiene así un significado ambivalente: el apartamiento físico o vivienda y el sentido de vida apartada, de *apartamiento*" (*El apartamiento* 109). The latter meaning of the word devalues their life for the protagonists. The very fact that they are forbidden to leave their apartment/prison makes them curious about what is outside. For the spectator, this curiosity reinforces the concept of interiorization, both physical and psychological. Indeed, the suggestions throughout the play are that this life apart is in fact a psychological dependence which the protagonists themselves have the power to break but which they dare not do because of their fear of what might happen to them.

At the end of the play, the spatial and temporal planes integrate to force the protagonists to confront their own complex identities and then to act accordingly. The inspectors, who have killed Terra and Lucío, leave Tlo, hands and feet bound, and order Carola and Elpidio to kill him. After the inspectors leave, the interior physical space from which fear allows no exit closes in on the two. To kill as they have been ordered forces a conscious act on their part. It also forces a mounting of tension for the spectator who recognizes this to be the first such act for these characters and who also knows the time for the play to end is very near.

Elpidio at first dominates their response by suggesting that they delay the murder, or in other words, do nothing. To do this would be analogous to their previous attempts to side-step the rules without really breaking them. But then Carola finally and decisively cuts the bonds, freeing the Indian. In this action, the positive affirmation of self takes precedence. Again, however, the emphasis is on the psychological rather than the physical confinement. Once freed, the Indian does nothing to liberate the protagonists, although he does say he will kill the inspectors. Symbolically, when the doorbell rings for the last time, there is hope for the protagonists since Carola has freed their historical awareness by her own actions.

Carola's decisiveness does not resolve the experience of the spectator, who is left at the end with his questions of what constitutes the reality of the play unanswered. Because no one aspect of the individual personalities seems to motivate openly Carola's action, one must now add the question of *why*? Reliance on thematic and chronological developments do not help in answering this question either since all semblances of objective reality prove to be false. For example, the tasks with which Carola and Elpidio busy themselves seem to lead to some definitive end. They do not. The order of arrival of things and people at the door seems to lead to a point where the play will reveal the answer to some central question. This perception is also false because when the bell rings for the last time in the play, it goes unanswered.

In the end, the spectator must rely on his/her own experience for any meaning to emerge. Since the background common to both spectator and characters is existence in a super-civilized society of physical conveniences, the viewer is led to contemplate the why's and wherefore's of the characters' existence, and by logical extension, of his own. René Marqués' words about Pirandello's "mirror theatre" illuminate the communication process in his own work as he says: "El hombre ante el espejo, o más exactamente, ante *su* espejo, el que ha de reflejar para él, en relámpago trágico de suprema lucidez, su imagen más posible auténtica, haciéndole comprender lo grotesco de su propia existencia y, por ende, de la de los demás. He ahí, en apretada síntesis, la razón de sus sinrazones conceptuales y técnicas dentro del teatro contemporáneo" (Marqués on Pirandello 36). The image one sees reflected here is composed of many subjective realities which form themselves in these characters' interiorized world. Taken as a whole they form only a very precarious reality since they seem to vie for dominance based on one's changing thoughts. In the end, the Indian Tlo is the catalyst which forces the protagonists to face themselves and to act in order to define their own identity in this subjective existence. The insistent doorbell at play's end, in a like manner, is the motivating element which forces the spectator to contemplate (not necessarily to define) his own reflected image in the projected world where fear of the unknown and a desire to affirm one's self identity compete for dominance.

Because of the ambiguity with which the play ends, the spectator, as a member of the 20th-century, "super-civilized society" of the West, must in the manner of which Brecht dreamed, analyze the entire play in its relationship to himself in order to see the meaning behind the message. The suggestions become clear that one lives multiple roles and that only by making and carrying out a decisive action can one affirm, and thus, create, one's own unique identity. In this specific case, Marqués refers to the uniqueness of the Spanish American, and of the Puerto Rican identity. However, whether it was the author's intent or not, the basic human dilemma of individuality succumbing to materialism and automation makes the universal nature of the work overshadow the more limited regional scope.

Although the European "Theatre of the Absurd" inspired René Marqués to write *La casa sin reloj* (1960); premiere in the Ateneo, 1961; published, 1962), this play does not appropriately belong to that tradition. Upon explaining his use of the term *absurdos* in place of *actos*, he claims the following:

> Todo comienza con la fatiga intelectual que me han causado los escritores europeos llamados de vanguardia en su empeño de dramatizar lo absurdo a través de una distorsión monstruosa de la realidad aparente, distorsión que afecta a personajes (rinocerontes y sillas en lugar de seres humanos), situaciones (un cadáver que crece, rompiendo paredes en algún suburbio londinés, por ejemplo) y lugares (basureros y zafacones en vez de salas, comedores y cuartos de dormir). "El Estreno de Esta Noche" 10)

He goes on to say there is no need to dramatize the absurd in contemporary man's life by resorting to such dehumanized symbols as those mentioned above; but rather that the absurd is to be found in the ordinary details of one's daily life. According to Marqués: "No es la realidad aparencial, sino la existencial la que el hombre de hoy ha distorsionado hasta el absurdo" (10). And, "en la vida actual, el absurdo se nos escurre en la rutina de cada día nuestro sin improbables monstruosidades, ni distorsiones de la realidad aparente, ni situaciones de inverosímil espectacularidad" (10).

The play, which takes place during the Nationalist insurrection of 1950, revolves around Micaela, a seemingly ordinary housewife of the middle class, "white-collar" society, who leads a trite and trivial life. The play's development concerns Micaela's attempts to reorganize her "safe" world when intruders threaten to destroy her self-created security. Two detectives, who come searching for revolutionaries, introduce the element of fear that goes with the break-up of one's established political and economic way of life. On this level, Micaela has stifled her own personal views and desires, and just as her husband Pedro feels secure in his job as a petty bureaucrat as long as he actively supports the dominant party politics, her place in society is safe as long as she is able to subdue her own feelings. This suppression of emotion has made her a non-feeling, non-caring, empty person. After the detectives' departure, the entrance of the Nationalist, José, threatens to destroy Micaela's self-created "safe" world both in terms of threats to her husband's position and destruction of the empty cold façade behind which she survives. The ensuing action portrays Micaela's and José's developing relationship as José instructs her in ways to value and appreciate life, including the redemptive quality of sacrificial love. In Micaela's twisted, self-devised logic, however, she decides that the only way to hold onto the love she comes to feel is through an act of sacrifice. In an ironic turn at the play's end, she applies her own extremist logic unrelentlessly to José's lessons and murders her new-found love. Thus, in her view, she gives herself the ability to experience the redeeming quality of feeling guilt.

La casa sin reloj creates the experience of the absurd within the inexorable passage of time which has the ability either to create or to destory meaning. The play presupposes a certain set of norms on the part of the spectator in relation to a twentieth-century, Western concept of time and to the logic, or lack of it, which one imposes on life within that context. The set of norms which govern the developing play are based on but in opposition to, those which the spectator presumably brings to his/her participatory role in the experience of this play. Through the tension resulting from this antagonism, the spectator, by nature of his/her presence and role, participates in the creation of the absurd while sharing Marqués' frustration and sense of urgency. Marqués has said:

> Cuando el espectador desconcertado o irritado por el final razonable exclame "¡Absurdo!", estará él o ella participando activamente (creadoramente, me atrevería a decir) en la perpetuación del absurdo en nuestra vida contemporánea. ("Estreno de Esta Noche" 10)

In this way, the dramatist creates artificially a set of specific circumstances which phenomenologically convey to the spectator the existentialist philosophy of that era.

The play's linear development depends on Micaela's frustrated attempts to search for meaning in herself and at the same time keep the security of her present reality. The imminent arrival and/or scenic interruption of Micaela's husband on several occasions creates and maintains the tension on stage while the audience's actual participation in the feeling of absurdity makes the work significant for the individual spectator.

The stage setting first prepares the spectator for the relationship between the absurd and the commonplace. The totally contiguous action takes place on the edge of a small town in a country house whose inhabitants are of the so-called "white-collar" middle class. According to the author's stage directions, there is nothing modern or noble about the houe whose furnishings are described as "extranjeros, vulgares y heterogéneos" (16). Artifical flowers and paintings of winter snow scenes, both inappropriate to the tropics, silently verify the absurdity of life in this place. The opening scene, during which the stage is empty, introduces the various factors which will be at work during the course of the play: the emptiness of Micaela's life; the sense of urgency which she feels and the audience experiences; and the intrusion into her security brought about because of the rebellion taking place on the Island. The spectator also experiences an intrusion inasmuch as his/her own expectations for what is happening are intruded upon.

Marqués uses the term *absurdo* as a noun to replace the more commonly-used *acto*. The *Webster's Dictionary* (New Collegiate, 1973) helps to illuminate for us the implications that the term has for this particular play. According to the Webster's, an *absurd* is "the state or condition in which man exists in an irrational and meaningless universe and in which man's life has no meaning outside his own existence" (5). In effect, each of the two acts, as well as what Marqués has called "a reasonable ending" correspond to this meaning of "absurd." That is, the play's characters exist within an irrational world, made meaningless by their own attempts to find significance in their respective situations. While the first "absurd" concentrates on Micaela's world, the second focuses on José's existentialist philosophy. These, in turn, are part of the larger "absurd" in which the spectator finds him/herself involved in a frustrating attempt to understand the reason and logic behind the play itself.

In the larger absurd, the spectator participates in a recurring pattern of ignorance—understanding—ignorance as he/she attempts to understand logically the sequence of events portrayed. Throughout, including the final scene in which Micaela finds great satisfaction in killing José, just as the spectator seems to have understood a particular situation or event, something will occur to undo that understanding.

Setting, characters, and situation, all contribute to the creation of the semblance of an irrational and meaningless world. Micaela's first appearance on stage, for example, in her uncombed hair and chenille house coat, contrasts sharply to a sensuous voice on the radio which the spectator has just heard advertising "Rose Petal Soap." The stage directions confirm what the audience will have witnessed: "Nada hay en ella que pueda hacernos confundirla con una estrella de cine, por lo que presumimos que el jabón que usa, no es, ciertamente, el mágico, embrujante y fascinante *Pétalo de Rosa*" (20). The visual contrast tells us that Micaela's "real" world is *not* that ideal one of the outside, a phone conversation that immediately follows confirms for us that her own *ideal* world is totally foreign to the *real* one of the outside.

The caller, who has reached a wrong number, is trying to ascertain the exact time. At this point, we see that Micaela's appearance does not reveal her true inner self. She responds first to the question by totally changing her appearance as a harried housewife. Her face becomes serene, her movements slow and deliberate. She is now on firm ground as she tells the caller she has no idea nor does she care what time it is. When the caller tells her that "time is money" she asks him what he would do if someone were to give him a check for the last two thousand years. And when he apologizes for having wasted her time, she responds: "¡Oh, no!, no me hace usted perder el tiempo. En el fondo. . . . Quiero decir, en el último análisis, no tengo tiempo alguno que perder" (22). As she hangs up the phone, she once again adopts "la máscara convencional de ama de casa atareada" (23). One must now realize that Micaela's own personal world corresponds neither to the idealized commercial realm nor to the so-called "real" world of "time is money," nor even to the seemingly stereotypical "harried housewife" world which she represents in appearance.

Time, in this play, is a silent, but powerful character whose influence manifests itself through the title, the actual playing time and the tempo which controls the sequencing of events. The title itself, *La casa sin reloj*, plays upon the spectator's own set of possessed norms of measuring time by suggesting a set of norms within the play tht are in opposition to those of the viewer. The title presupposes a certain view of time. *The House without a Clock* assumes that this type of dwelling, because it is a rarity, will seem interesting to its audience, for whom the more common house would be one *with* a clock. This indispensable instrument for measuring the passage of minutes and hours has a much greater cultural function than its simple mechanical one, for it codifies our daily comings and goings, connects us to other human beings, controls our decisions, and ultimately reminds us of the tenuousness of life.

If the title presumes to go against the norm, the subtitle, "Comedia antipoética en dos absurdos y un final razonable," supposedly affirms the spectator's reaction to the title. This would certainly be an illogical situation in the world contemporary to the play's events. Moreover, the title characterizes the protagonist, Micaela, as a persona whose inner logic is diametrically opposed to that which the spectator can be assumed to accept as the norm. We see the establishment of this position in her phone conversation and in a later discussion with José when José says there is still time for her to comb her hair before her husband arrives and she responds: "¿Quién se ocupa del tiempo?" (43). Or when she tells José that "No hay reloj en esta casa" (52).

While the title and the characterization of Micaela indicate the thematic importance of time in the work, the actual passage of time creates the underlying tension which rules both the characters and the spectators. Differently from most of Marqués' dramatic works, in *La casa sin reloj*, the actual playing time is exactly the same as the dramatic time of the characters. The play itself becomes a clock in that time is very strictly measured and uncontrolled by any element within the play. In its most recently published version, the work begins with the voice of the radio commercial and an empty stage. However, the original version began somewhat differently and significantly enlightens us about the play's dramatic unfolding. According to José Lacomba, the first edition text reads as follows at the beginning of the stage directions to Act One:

> The theatre is dark. Before the curtain rises, there is the strong tick-tick of a great alarm clock. Then the bells of the clock give the hour. As the third bell is heard, a powerful masculine voice is heard.
>   Man's Voice:—Stop the time! (*Three or four seconds of absolute silence follows.*)
>   Man's Voice:—(*Louder, almost inhuman.*) Why a clock in a world filled with the absurd? (Lacomba, 22)

Whatever the reasons might be for the omission of this opening from later editions of the play, the fact remains that the passage faithfully reflects the temporal elements at work here. The first act serves to present a world in which time has, in effect, "stopped," at least for Micaela. However, it also provides a clue as to the link between this stopping of time and the absurdity which Micaela sees in the outside world. For example, one absurdity with which Micaela co-exists is the fact that her husband's lover often calls him at home. This fact in itself is perhaps not absurd, but Micaela's way of responding to it is. She explains the logic to José: "¡Pues a dónde va a llamarlo! ¿No es ésta la casa de mi marido?" (48). A further explanation clarifies her actions as she says:

> Para que algo trajera la felicidad tendría que suceder una de dos cosas. . . . Fíjese: el mundo tendría que dejar de ser lo absurdo que es. O, si eso es imposible, uno tendría que aceptar lo absurdo que es el mundo con naturalidad tal, como si no se percibiera su . . . absurdidad. . . . (4)

As the play develops and finally culminates in Micaela's final act of protecting her world, it becomes clear that the latter direction is the one Micaela has followed. To accept the absurd as natural, however, she has had to sacrifice her own ability to experience any kind of human emotions. With feeling abolished, time has no significance in her meaningless existence.

The second act (actually beginning with the arrival of Micaela's husband, Pedro, at the very end of the first) introduces another function of time in which it is imbued with a dramatic life of its own. Through a series of intrusions, time begins to tick away as the play itself becomes the clock that measures that ticking. Thus, the feelings of urgency and fear that underlie Micaela's actions and to an extent of lesser emphasis, those of José, are communicated to the spectator creating the dramatic tension which commands our attention.

The sense of urgency that grows into the tension of the second act is evident in the play's opening scene in which Micaela first appears in the background chaos of the radio announcer and the knocks on the door. Both continue until she turns the radio off. Just as she starts to answer the door and thus put an end to the supposed chaos, the telephone rings, adding still more urgency to the created tension. As a result of her decision to answer the phone rather than the door, the knocks continue incessantly throughout the ensuing conversation.

At the end of Act One, Pedro's imminent arrival re-establishes the phenomenological urgency since José's presence potentially may cause several problems: he has entered illegally, he is a Nationalist, and he is alone with Pedro's wife, just to mention the more important potential problems. The sound of Pedro's horn initiates a scene in which Micaela and José frantically search for an explanation for the latter's prsence. When Pedro finally does enter, he does not at first even notice the intruder. When he does, the awaited surprise reaction on Pedro's part does not occur but rather, it is the spectator who is surprised with Pedro's "Tú" (58). Obviously the two know each other, so it is Micaela and the spectator who are surprised, and not Pedro. The tension of waiting has been re-directed to force the viewer's participation in the experience.

The second act begins with the exact words with which the first act ends, communicating contiguity of time and action. However, in this second act, the notion of tempo takes over and Pedro's repeated intrusions on the scene simulate the ticking of the clock as time slips away, forcing Micaela's final action. This act actually consists of one long intense conversation between José and Micaela in which he instructs her in his philosophical view of life and during which time the two fall in love. Pedro's presence, however, at three different points and his subsequent departure section the conversation and build the tension at the same time. He has left the scene to take a cold shower and is seen leaving the shower with a towel wrapped around him. He reappears wearing his robe with the towel around his neck. Finally, he enters fully dressed. Each step is a logical one in any chronology of bathing, thus signifying the minute by minute passage of time. In this way time, while unmeasured in Micaela's world, still continues to pass unrelentlessly as part of the spectator's experience.

The juxtaposition of Pedro's final appearance to a phone conversation between José and the Central Telephone Office emphasizes the tension at work here and creates a point at which the tension begins to intensify rapidly. José calls the Central Office to find out what time it is but discovers that all clocks stopped at 3 o'clock. In effect, time appears to have stopped. Pedro's immediate appearance tells us otherwise, though, and he finally threatens to turn his brother in to the police.

With this threat, the play's tempo in relation to the urgency of the situation speeds up. Micaela enters with a gun supposedly ready to kill her husband and thus protect her new-found relationship with José. After Pedro leaves, possibly to turn José in, or possibly to buy his passage out of the country (it is impossible to know which) José enters into the final stage of instruction. He tells Micaela that "love" is the key in her search for her ability to feel guilt. he says: "Hasta que en el Paraíso no se tuvo conciencia del amor, no hubo pecado ni culpa. Ni conocimiento del tiempo siquiera, de lo inexorable que es para el hombre el tiempo. Hasta entonces no hubo posibilidad de redención" (94).

As the tension grows, José lures Micaela into feeling love and its full significance. In an emotional scene, Micaela faints and when she wakes, she seems to be in the world which José lives. She finally feels the passage of time when she says:

> Micaela—¿No oye usted esas campanadas?
> José—¿Campanadas?
> Micaela—¡Es un reloj!
> José—No hay reloj en esta casa.
> Micaela—(*Nerviosa.*) Es cierto. (*Atemorizada.*) Está ocurriendo algo aquí. ¿No lo siente usted? Tengo miedo. ¡Dios mío! No entiendo. (*En grito súbito.*) José, sálveme usted. (96)

Micaela's fear grows correspondingly to the love between her and José. She now feels that she must know the hour and upon learning that it is impossible because all the clocks have stopped working, she approaches a state of panic. The tempo again picks up when she claims: "Nunca sabremos el tiempo que hemos pasado juntos. Es espantoso. Vendrán, vendrán a llevarte. Ya Pedro te habría delatado. (*Aterrada.*) ¡Tienes que irte!" (98). At this very moment, knocks are heard on the door, seemingly confirming her fears. The tension is alleviated somewhat at this point since it is only a bill delivery and not the police. The episode, however, introduces the element of imminent death into the denouement and prepares the final step in Micaela's learning process. In response to Micaela's insistence that José *cannot* die, he says to her: "Todos *podemos* morir. Mejor aún, todos *debemos* morir. Siempre ha de morir alguien para dar vida a otro ser" (101). From here to the end, Micaela is much more sure of herself and she insists that they must use the revolver to defend themselves. She fears if she loses José her old world will return. Finally, after convincing hm to teach her how to shoot, she kills him. The play ends as Micaela calls the police confessing her guilt, which she is now able to feel. As the curtain falls, a clock chimes the hour.

Playing with time re-creates for the spectator Micaela's experience of frustration and urgency. By suppressing time, Micaela does not have to deal with the world which she fears. Instrusions into her created reality start the clock as she moves with the play toward an eventual confrontation with that world. Her love for the intruder, José, ironically becomes the force that allows her to murder him in order for her to live once again in the greater world. His presence offers her a choice between love and guilt, while the play itself serves as a clock ticking away until Micaela must make the choice. The spectator, who experiences the same sense of urgency (although for a different reason) may not be able to accept Micaela's choice at the end, but must at least contemplate how that choice is related to the fear of change.

Both of these plays emphasize the absurdities of life without becoming "theatre of the absurd" in the strictest sense. They concentrate on one's dependence on fear of change within a somewhat secure but very limiting existence. In *El apartamiento*, past, present, and future coexist in a future space with no exit for the two protagonists as long as they conform to the rules and are afraid to think and act on their own. The instant they do, they literally and figuratively begin to open the door to some kind of hopeful life for themselves. The multiple roles with which the two main characters are associated throughout the play's development serve as the catalyst which causes the spectator to contemplate just what constitutes the identity of an individual and the significance that acceptance of that identity might have for the future.

La casa sin reloj plays on the viewer's own concept of time while creating a sense of urgency from the tension between a supposed suppression of time and the obvious passage of time. The urgency experienced by the spectator is parallel to that which the protagonist feels as she futilely tries to have the best of two worlds: her own safe, non-feeling, non-caring secure existence, and her newly discovered love for the intruder in her house. In the end, she is only able to survive by assassinating her love and living with the guilt her action brings.

In both works, the characters' ways of resolving their dilemma send a message about making choices and expressing one's true feelings in today's world rather than opting for self-repression and greater security.

Chapter VII

Timeless Power/Powerful Time:
The Cinema on Stage

Throughout history, the theatre has developed and assimilated esthetically novel techniques in order to give a new brilliance to those already established. One such technique adapted to the theatre is the imitation of cinematography as a means of artistic expression. This assimilation of the cinema is most obvious in techniques of scenic production. The theatrical imitation of film was first employed significantly in the expressionistic theatre of the twenties and thirties, especially in the productions of the Provincetown Players with whom Eugene O'Neill's name is often mentioned. According to author Susan Sontag, one way in which the expressionist theatre incorporated cinematic techniques was the utilization of lighting media to isolate the actor or a part of a scene, or upon darkening sections of the stage. And, when it uses the revolving stage, according to Sontag, the theatre approximates the instantaneous displacement that one obtains through the camera ("Film and Theatre" 372). As a result, the Twentieth-Century dramatist has acquired tremendous power in translating his/her creative imagination to the medium of the stage.

René Marqués experimented with and incorporated new techniques such as these into his dramatic literature and it is possible to point out in his work techniques specifically related to film. Indeed, the dramatist called special attention to the cinematic qualities of his last three plays: *Sacrificio en el Monte Moriah* (1969) and *David y Jonatán/Tito y Berenice* (1970). Marqués qualifies the former play as a "drama en catorce escenas cinematográficas" (*Sacrificio en el Monte Moriah* 5) while insisting that the scene changes in the latter twin plays be effected rapidly with no time lapse nor intermission between, as if they were scenic changes in a movie. In all three plays the particular use of lighting and stage space creates the illusion of disjointed spaces and allows for the traversing of greater time spans while focusing the spectator's attention on the thematic aspects of the works.

A close examination of Marqués' scenic directions in *Sacrificio en el Monte Moriah* clearly reveals what he understood to be "cinematographic techniques" in his text. He insists on cinematic fluidity in the theatrical presentation. To achieve it, he employs lighting techniques to create the illusion of discontinuity in the scenification and to create the effect of close-ups. Moreover, he demands "perfect synchronization" between action, illumination, and sound.

The fluidity and the order of the scenes, the close-ups, and the imitation of cinematic space upon the stage create the illusion that we are in the presence of a film. In order to understand the use of these techniques, we must ask ourselves what is the result of adapting cinematographic techniques to the theatre, specifically in the case of Marqués' work. For Stanley Kracauer, "Cinematography . . . aims at transforming the agitated spectator into a conscious observer" ("The Establishment of Physical Existence" 277). We can see in these three plays how Marqués achieves a similar effect in his theatre. Using the cinema's recourses, he tightly controls the spectator's attention, changing him from being merely a passive witness to some dramatic scenes to the more active role through which he perceives the significance the work has for today's world. In his role as conscientious observer, the spectator understands that the use of violence—whether it be physical or mental—to maintain power, results in the sacrifice of others and that it is just as thematically valid in the 20th century as in the Biblical era.

Sacrificio en el Monte Moriah is an interpretation of the Biblical story of the patriarch, Abraham, his wife, Sara, and their son, Issac. It is one in which the author alters the traditional relationships creating a weak and cowardly patriarch who prostitutes his wife for his own benefit, and who is willing to sacrifice his son in exchange for material comforts. Abraham, obsessed with his god Yahvé, interprets his deity based upon his own personal necessities. At the same time, he becomes so submissive before his god that he transforms himself into a person without criteria and without feelings. In order to maintain his position of power, he resorts to dehumanizing violence without considering the price others will pay for his actions. Abraham's attitude will return to him in the form of an ironic vengeance for which he will have to pay at the end of his life. Through the actions of Abraham and those of Sara, the work establishes a parallel between physical and passive violence. Sara's on-stage murdering of her husband represents a passionate and physical violence. On the other hand a passive violence is seen in the cold and calculated actions of the patriarch when he turns his wife over to other men, when he circumcises his son, and finally, when he attempts to sacrifice his son at Yahvé's altar. The sacrificial knife symbolizes both kinds of violence which in the end destroy authentic values such as love, and make impossible the development of a personal identity for Abraham's progeny.

Cinema critics agree that it is the *montage* that instills meaning in a film. According to critic André Bazin, the montage is "the ordering of images in time" ("The Evolution of the Language of Cinema" 124), and it is "the creation of a sense or meaning not proper to the images themselves but derived exculsively from their juxtaposition" (126). When we examine Marqués' work in accordance to Bazin's theory, we see that the dramatist imparts a new meaning to the Biblical events dramatized by use of a scenic *montage* that imitates that of the cinema. The author has insisted in the stage directions that the performance be without intermissions between acts: "La obra debe fluir ininterrumpidamente de escena a escena durante el tiempo aproximado que dura una película de metraje normal" (18). By means of this uninterrupted flow, the work guides the spectator along a single path from which he is not permitted to stray; thus controlling what will be the focus of the spectator's attention.

The montage of this work consists of fourteen scenes with the action developing in two different time periods: first, the fictionalized present of the work; and second, the historical events interpreted by Marqués from the Biblical story. Each scene is structurally complete in itself but all fourteen taken together give unity to the work's climax. The first four scenes alternate between the present in which Sara is at the point of killing Abraham (I and III), and the remote past of the story in which Abraham gives Sara as a gift to the Pharoah, a calulated action which the patriarch takes in order to protect himself and his own position. The next six scenes, presented from the historical perspective, develop mainly around the alleged sons of Abraham, Ishmael and Isaac, and conclude in the scenes in which Abraham takes Isaac to Mount Moriah to sacrifice him according to Yahvé's orders. The last four scenes present the aborted sacrifice, Sara's appearance in which she disguises herself as an angel in order to prevent her son's murder, and finally the destruction of the marriage, the family, and of Abraham himself, at the hands of his wife, who kills him with the sacrificial knife.

The omission of intermissions and the rapid scene transitions heighten the effectiveness of the work's denouement, creating a celerity which guides the spectator to concentrate on the events themselves, and thus subconsciously to subordinate the temporal element to the work's thematics. The events dramatized are those which best highlight the theme of sacrifice and violence and perhaps for that reason, Marqués does not recount in detail the historical elements. Although the work treats an historical subject, the total presentation projects an aura of atemporality. The opening scene, conducted in darkness, involves the spectators in the theme from the beginning when they are turned the color of blood by several "blood-red" spotlights from different angles of the proscenium and the house. A prophetic voice speaks to the audience:

> ¡Ay, llorad; llorad y sangrad por vosotros mismos que vais siempre a Egipto en busca de ayuda, porque no sabéis encontrarla en el fondo de vuestros propios corazones! (5)

In this speech we see how Marqués, speaking directly to the spectator, forces the viewer to evaluate his/her own being and circumstance whether that be the specific situation of Puerto Rico or the more universal circumstance of the human being confronted by a materialistic world and by powerful, unscrupulous persons. In the more specific case of Puerto Rico a parallel exists between Egypt and the United States. Egypt in the play, and the United States in Puerto Rican reality, are major powers where one goes in search of aid without considering the cost to be paid by submission in exchange for economic wealth.

The manner in which Marqués uses scenic space also creates the illusion that the play is a film. Sontag distinguishes theatrical space from cinematic space in the following way:

> Theatre is confined to a logical or *continuous* use of space. Cinema (through editing, that is, through the change of shot—which is the basic unit of film construction) has access to an alogical or *discontinuous* use of space. In the theatre, people are either in the stage space or "off." When "in," they are always visible or visualizable in contiguity with each other. In the cinema, no such relation is necessarily visible nor visualizable. (366)

In the presentation of *Sacrificio en el Monte Moriah*, Marqués creates the illusion of discontinuity of space and time at the level of the scene.

According to José Lacomba, who designed the stage set for the production of this work in the Culture Institute's Thirteenth Annual Theatre Festival: "a rotating stage is the ideal theatrical structure for the cinematographic changes that Marqués asks for in his play" ("The Man and the Dramatist" n.p.). However, when the work was staged in the Tapia Theatre, there was no rotating stage and so Lacomba opted for a series of multi-level platforms, utilized indiscriminately. The use of these platforms when coordinated with the illumination, produced a scenic fludity reminiscent of cinematic celerity.

Each scene develops in a different space and the only scene in which we see the full stage is the second, which occurs in the Egyptian Pharoah's Court. In his instructions to the work's director, Marqués emphasizes the necessity of isolating each scene within its own space from the others. Marqués says: "Si el equipo de luminotécnico no es adecuado y no se logra oscurecimiento total en las otras plataformas mientras se desarrolla la acción en una de ellas, se sugiere que cada plataforma—aquellas donde pueda utilizarse—tenga su propio e independiente telón" (153). This isolating of the scenes gives fluidity and unity to the montage. In this way, the play flows naturally and the spectator does not miss a detailed exposition in the development of the story line. Instead, he/she is now able to direct his/her attention and imagination to the sacrifice related to the implicit socio-political structure. The viewer's efforts are directed away from the chronology of familiar events and re-focused upon the humanistic values which underlie the work's communication system.

The use of some tricks and visual effects, including black-outs, a "knife dance," and close-ups created by the use of spotlights, communicates the applicability of the work's theme to today's life. One could go so far as to say that the close relationship among the visual effects creates the work's dramatic structure. In the total darkness of the first scene, weapons of several categories stand out, with prominence given to the sacrificial knife. They are bladed weapons which appear to be put into action by invisible hands: "Todas las armas blancas . . . proceden a ejecutar movimientos lentos y rítmicos en ataques y golpes mortales como si se tratase de un baile o ballet autónomo, sin intervención de manos humanas. . . ." (17). This dance, synchronized with a loud burst of thunder, establishes the concepts of sacrifice and violence. The weapons become immobilized, followed by the words of two sentinels:

VOZ DE HOMBRE I—¡Centinela! ¿Qué has visto en la noche?
VOZ DE HOMBRE II—He visto venir, esperanzada . . . la mañana. (57)

These hopeful speeches will take on a greater significance for the
spectator at the end of the work. As the work flows from scene to
scene, the viewer arrives at an understanding of the work's paradox
primarily through the accumulation of impressions of sacrifice and
violence.

The close-ups in Scenes I and III are reflections of the knife
dance, to which are added more specifically the element of human
intervention. Béla Belázs says of the close-up: "When the film close-up
strips the veil of our imperceptiveness and insensitivity from the
hidden little things, and shows us the face of objects, it still shows us
man, for what makes objects expressive are the human expressions
projected onto them. The objects only reflect our own selves. . . . " ("The
Face of Man" 290). The close-ups which Marqués designs are at once
visual images of sacrifice and violence, and a message that reveals the
cause and effect relationship between the comportment of one generation and that of another. Scene XI treats the sacrifice of Isaac on Mount
Moriah. When Abraham raises the sacrificial knife in his hand in order
to carry out the sacrifice "surge un foco de luz blanca que toma en
'close-up' la inmovilizada mano en alto de Abrahán con el cuchillo
cuya hoja brilla siniestramente" (115). Immediately there is a total
black-out except for the spot which isolates the hand and the knife. In
this way, one forgets momentarily the identity of the person who
raises the knife, but not his humanness. And so, for a few seconds, the
temporal limits between the specific historical action and the spectator
are erased.

This close-up is repeated parallely in Scene XIII, which presents
the family's last meal, at which time Isaac rejects his parents and their
"ideals." In this scene, the knife is in Isaac's hand and is not raised as
in the earlier scene, but rather, it is offered to Abraham, with the
invitation that the pariarch again attempt to spill blood as he did on
Mount Moriah. By creating a relationship between these two scenes
by means of the close-up, Marqués emphasizes the perpetration of
sacrifice and the result that such an action holds for the victim (in this
case, Isaac). Isaac leaves his parents saying: "No quiero pertenecer
más a esta familia abominable. No quiero ser más cómplice en la total
destrucción de este pueblo de esclavos que ni siquiera saben que lo
son" (135). In this confrontation, Isaac (symbolizing for Marqués

Puerto Rico) rejects *both* parents' ideals, in deference to the maintaining of his own identity.

The last scene unites the work's dramatic circle as it returns to the present. The knife appears once again, this time in Sara's hand as she is about to kill Abraham. According to her, the action is for her people's own salvation. This time, the close-up is not on the weapon but on Sara's face, illuminated by a blood-red light, and making of her both victim and heroine. The work returns to its beginning as all lights are extinguished while an enormous sacrificial knife stained with blood descends into center stage. Once again the voices of the sentinels are heard repeating the same words as in Scene I, but with a textual change that terminates the work and completes its meaning:

> VOZ DE HOMBRE (Ampliada).—He visto venir, con horror . . . , *el* mañana. (14)

The voice and the knife's appearance are synchronized with a "blood red" light which invades the area where the knife is, and one hears in the background a Chorus lamenting. These elements, together with the changes in the sentinel's words "esperanzado" for "con horror" and "la mañana" for "*el* mañana," alert the spectator to a warning that is at the same time a prediction for the present era, since the epoch in which the spectator lives is the future in relation to the Biblical history. Marqués very appropriately prefaces the play with the Biblical phrase: "No hay nada nuevo bajo el sol" (Ecclesiastes).

Marqués offers three possible solutions to today's spectator: first, to be like Abraham and lose oneself for the sake of maintaining a certain level of material life without humanitarian ideals; second, to act as does Sara and destroy the instrument of violence, responding to violence with violence; or, third, to dare, as does Isaac, to reject the other two possibilities completely then to begin *a tabula rasa* to become who one really is. Sara says of Isaac's choice: "Isaac ya es libre. Libre de ti, de mí, de Yahvé . . . ¡Libre al fin!" (135). This is freedom as Marqués conceives it in his total body of work; it is not merely a political or social freedom, but rather a freeing of oneself from oneself—from the fear of following one's own desires and of searching for (and perhaps finding) one's true identity.

With the structure which Marqués achieves in this work, scenic space and lighting create the illusion of a cinematic celerity, thus making the theme stand out through the dramatized events. Visual coordination establishes a relationship between the various scenes and the viewer, who, upon realizing that it is he/she who lives "*el mañana*" in the work and that it is he/she who sacrifices the authentic human values in exchange for a materialistic life, becomes aware of the seriousness and transcendence of Marqués' message.

René Marqués gave his other two Biblically based plays, *David y Jonatán, Tito y Berenice* the single subtitle "dos dramas de amor, poder y desamor" and he insisted that they be published and performed together as if they were one work (Vásquez Alamo, prologue, 10). For that reason, I have chosen to treat them as one unit. The appearance at the front of each text of the Biblical quotation from the first chapter of "Ecclesiastes," verse nine, "Lo que fue, siempre será, lo que se hizo, lo mismo se hará; nada hay de nuevo bajo el sol" (17) forms a further link between the two plays. Despite the fact that each work is capable of standing alone as far as the story presented is concerned, taken as one, they become a single parable illustrating the introductory quote. The editor, F. Vázquez Alamo, has called the two works "una estremecedora parábola del mundo actual" (Prologue, 7).

David y Jonatán, based upon the famous Biblical friendship, emphasizes the destruction of that bond between the two youths at the hands of the political maneuverings of Samuel, the last judge-priest of Israel who, in Marqués' version, never relinquishes his control over the kings he chooses for his people. In this modification of the famous story, authentic feelings are constantly frustrated by obedience to power, in this case, tightly controlled by Samuel. A youthful Saul, happily in love and devoted to his wife and family, reluctantly becomes the first king of Israel. We next see him fifteen years later, a melancholy old man, whose children, *Jonatán* and *Mikol,* are afraid to approach him and from whom he has distanced himself as king to the point of destroying any real communication with them.

The miraculous appearance of the young David, whose beauty and naturalness cause Saul and his two children to love the youth, re-establishes momentarily the idyllic and naive love at which Saul hinted at the play's beginning. Once again, however, Samuel and his constant companion, power, step in to destroy the idyll, as the spectator learns in retrospect that the old judge-priest has sent David to the palace and has already annointed him as the "future" king of Israel, prior to Saul's seeing him for the first time. Finally, Samuel creates political animosity between the two friends, Jonathan and David, a situation which forces Jonathan to challenge his friend David. Although David tries to avoid the fight, he accidentally kills his friend and so fulfills Samuel's wishes as he murders his only chance at love. In the final scene Samuel appears, as David laments the death of his friend and rightful king. The author's stage directions describe the authority which political power has in this play via the character Samuel: "Sonríe de modo enigmático, mirando el cadáver de Saúl a sus pies y sabiendo él con nosotros que detrás de cada 'trono' habrá siempre un 'juez-sacerdote' " (55).

Tito y Berenice treats the same theme of power as destroyer of love but in this work the inexorable passage of time itself fulfills the role of villain that Samuel plays in the former. The play opens with a love scene between Tito, the son of the Roman Emporer, and Berenice, daughter of Herod Agrippa, the last king of Judea. This scene, rather than illuminating any true feelings of love between the two, focuses on the obstacles to their relationship created by each of their political circumstances. The second and third scenes, occurring in the plot line prior to the first, make clear the underlying motives. Berenice has gone, at her father's insistence, to avenge her people through her beauty. Tito, who spares her life despite his own orders to leave no Judean alive, succumbs to her supposed plot of revenge by falling in love with her. After spending a year living with the Judean princess as her husband, Tito is called to Rome where he will become Emporer. To do so, he must renounce his marriage in order to comply with Roman law, and take a Roman wife. He leaves Berenice behind to wait for him, promising to return as soon as possible. The remainder of the play, alternating between Italy and Judea, reveals the contrast between Tito's very public life and his growing subservience to his own power on the one hand, and Berenice's life as a captive princess who grows old waiting for her lover's return on the other. When Tito finally does return, after many years, with the blessing of the Roman Senate, time has stolen Berenice's youth and beauty and the possibility of any authentic love between them. As in the first play, the hold that power has on the individual is ultimately responsible for the death of love.

Both works portray power as a force that seduces and then traps the hopeful youth so that they may not respond to their own personal feelings and desires free of the political circumstances surrounding them. When we examine the two plays together, however, as a single entity, the primary focus shifts away from the power vs. love conflict and centers on the proverb which introduces each play and which Berenice recites near the end. "There is nothing new under the sun," mankind continues to make the same errors from generation to generation and, in this case, from era to era. Logically, meaning emerges from the relationship which the spectator perceives between the two works as they are juxtaposed in their performance. It is the technical presentation that makes possible this perception. Both plays create the illusion of cinematographic celerity through the discontinuous use of space and time, traversing great distances and time spans. At the same time, the similarity in the structures of the two works strengthens the continuity between the events portrayed.

Tension, in both works, arises from the constant antagonism between the individual and one's supposed responsibility to a political reality. This tension becomes the focal point of each play as it is reflected in specific events as well as in the temporal and spatial elements and the pattern of events that develops. All of these factors combine with the illusion of cinematic celerity to sharpen the spectator's consciousness of the underlying message suggested by the Biblical proverb.

In each play, we see power as a force that corrupts and manipulates the individual's own personal feelings and tendencies. In *David y Jonatán*, the judge-priest, Samuel, first warns his naive Israeli public as well as his unaware theatre public of the dangers of power. In Scene I, an invisible public demands a human king such as other nations have. Although his followers are never aware, Samuel implies that the immediate threat of the Phillistines whom they fear is not as great as that of a human king. He warns them: "Un rey humano os traerá muchas tribulaciones" (22), but finally gives in to their demand with the final warning: "Os aseguro que si lo queréis, nustro pueblo tendrá un rey . . . un rey humano como otras naciones. (*Un sutil acento de amenaza en su voz.*) Con todas sus consecuencias" (22). His people respond to this with shouts of joy, leaving the theatre audience the task of wondering about Samuel's meaning.

In addition to playing the role of clairvoyant, the corrupt Samuel comes to be the power-force that corrupts the puppet-like characters in this work. He encounters Saul in a rapid scene change after promising his people a human king. Saul, who is somewhat of a weakling and certainly not of the stature of a king, is finally overcome by Samuel's prophetic vision. Samuel points out to Saul that as king he will have more than physical strength. He prophesies: "Pero, tú tendrás mucha más fuerza. (*Cerrando los ojos.*) Y tus descendientes la tendrán más y más . . . sobre la tierra. Y será mucho más tierra. Aunque cueste ríos de sangre. . . ." (25). Saul finally attempts to escape his destiny as Samuel tells it, but to no avail. He resists by saying: "Respeto tu sabiduría y tu condición de profeta, venerable Samuel. ¡Pero no quiero oír más! Vuelvo a la tierra de mi padre. (*Va a salir. Le detiene la voz terriblemente profética de* Samuel.) ¡Detente, Saúl, hijo de Kis! ¡Yahvé así lo ha ordenado! (*Pausa.*) Serás el rey primero del pueblo de Israel" (25). The rapid darkening of the stage and the immediate scene change to Saul's coronation convey to the spectator the failure of Saul's resistence. The missing details of what must have occurred are unimportant since it is Saul's failure to resist Samuel's power which is the intended center of attention.

A similar relationship exists between Samuel and David, whom Samuel annoints as future king before the youth has any understanding of the circumstances. Once David has developed a friendship with Jonathan, the legitimate heir to the throne, he forms his own opinion and protests Samuel's prior action. Samuel responds always from his power: "Soy aún sumo sacerdote. Y fui supremo juez antes de yo mismo instaurar la monarquía. Déjame a mí las cuestiones de derecho . . . divinas y humanas. Tú, hasta que aprendas a gobernar, dedícate a la guerra" (44). To perpetuate his own control over David, the future king, Samuel names Saul himself as the enemy. David's only response is to fall on his knees horrified and to cover his eyes as he shouts "¡No!" (44). The omission of elaborated details and the immediate darkening of the stage indicate the impossibility of David's doing anything except what Samuel orders.

Obedience to power at the expense of personal needs likewise interrupts and, through the passage of time, destroys Tito Flavio's personal desire to live as Berenice's husband and at the same time, makes of her life a death-like existence. In this play, Rome, meaning the Roman Senate and Empire, is the power-force that demands obedience. After having spent one year in Judea with Berenice as his legal wife, Tito, upon his father's death, must return to Rome to become Emperor, renouncing his marriage to Berenice. His explanation to his wife reveals the tension between the personal and political interests: "¡Oh, Berenice, Berenice! Hice todo lo imaginable por mantener nuestro matrimonio en secreto. Pero Roma oye, Roma todo lo ve . . . Roma todo lo sabe" (72). With these words, Tito reveals two important ideas to the viewers: one, Tito's awareness of the potential conflict, revealed by the fact that he tried to keep his marriage to a former political enemy secret; and, two, the concept of Rome as an omniscient force in the face of which Tito appears to be powerless.

As Tito's own political influence grows, power is seen as a corrupting force which gives him the courage to abandon his total dedication to Rome by taking a mistress, ignoring his duties of government so that he is neither true to himself and his promise to Berenice nor to his political duties. Power, now in a different form, turns him back to an awareness of his political responsibilities and at the same instant makes him aware of his personal responsibilities. In Scene VII, the most ornate and elaborated of the ten, Tito, while at his country palace, witnesses a dance reminiscent of the "Dance of Seven Veils" performed by seven Jewish dancers. The principal dancer, whom we associate with Berenice, wears a gold mask. She disrobes completely except for the mask and at the point of her removing it, Mount Vesuvius (seen in the background) erupts, killing Tito's mistress and destroying the palace. Tito interprets the two events as a warning to him from the gods and promises to reform:

> "Si me perdonáis, seré fiel a Roma inmortal y no a mis mortales debilidades. (Se deja caer de rodillas.) Todo aquel error que he cometido, lo rectificaré. (Toma la máscara de oro de la bailarina no identificada quien la dejó caer en la caótica desbandada.) A todo aquel a quien he herido, pediré mi perdón. (Lleva la máscara a sus labios.) Todo lo que he quitado, lo restituiré. (Casi para sí.) Berenice. . . ." (87)

Here the curtain falls, leaving the spectator to contemplate the still unresolved antagonism. Tito recognizes the conflict between his political duties and his personal feelings but by clinging to his desire for Berenice, does not resolve the two antagonistic forces.

In each work, the time element itself also reflects the personal and the political power forces as antagonists. It is especially revealed in the relationship between generations and in the unrelentless presence of a destructive force. In David y Jonatán, the young Jonathan, who represents the purest, most authentic feelings of love, is also the primary political hope for the continuance of his father's reign. Both Tito and Berenice represent the continuance of a family line insomuch as they are children of kings and in terms of their actions as well. The constant presence of Samuel in the first play symbolically becomes synonomous with power as he manipulates, over the course of several years, each of the characters as if they had no will of their own. In Tito y Berenice, a similar role is played by the passage of time, symbolized in the veil which always covers Berenice's lost youth and beauty, conveying both that loss as well as Tito's inability to recognize it.

Scene VII of *David y Jonatán* firmly establishes Jonathan's purity and the true feeling of love for him that both his sister, Mikol, and his friend, David, feel. These latter two observe from the palace window the nude Jonathan, and while doing so, comment in litany form on his beauty:

> MIKOL.—*(Dejando de reir.)* Ya sale. ¡Es hermoso su cuerpo!
> DAVID.—*(Quien ya no ríe.)* Lo es. Como una copa sagrada.
> MIKOL.—Como un dios de las aguas.
> DAVID.—Como una estatua de oro que Yahvé ... no nos permite tocar.
> MIKOL.—*(Mirando hacia lo alto.)* Como el sol cuando hace refulgir la piel diamantina de Jonatán, ¡deslumbrante!
> DAVID.—*(Mirando hacia el vacío.)* Como la luna, cuando de noche se enreda en los cabellos de cobre del Sinaí de Jonatán, ¡tan distante! (41)

This litany sets Jonathan up as the most authentic and most loved pesonage—and the most appropriate victim. His own purity conveys the pureness of the feelings of the other two youth. The litany also sets up the slightest hint of an intense love between Jonathan and David as David sees a god-like being who is untouchable. Later in the same scene, Samuel interrupts the two young men in an embrace. However, Samuel does not react to it as anything other than normal. This reaction, juxtaposed to the intensity and purity of the feelings conveyed by all three young people tends to emphasize the naturalness and the credibility of the love, rather than a negative societal view of the relationship.

Jonathan's purity is compromised, however, by his political responsibilities as son of the king and legal heir to the throne. As Saul dies, having committed suicide, he says from an empty stage: "¡Jonatán! ¡Tú eres la esperanza mía, y la venganza, además!" (51). In fact, Jonathan's final loyalty to his political obligations brings about his death. In a duel with a reluctant David, whom he sees as his political rival for the throne, Jonathan trips on his father's royal robe which he now wears, and David kills him accidentally.

The constant, almost eternal, presence of Samuel, as symbol of power, is another temporal element which reflects the central antagonistic forces and underscores the impossibility of the coexistence of love and power as well. Samuel himself is corrupt because of his own obsession with power. He makes his hypocrisy quite clear as he responds to his Acolyte's doubts about the change of the form of government from the judge-priest rule to a monarchy. The Acolyte asks if this concludes the power of the judge-priests and Samuel answers:

> En cierta medida . . . si lo crees así . . . Pero entiende que detrás del trono siempre habrá un sacerdote, que también será juez . . . Saúl, Saúl, primer rey de los israelitas. Para mi sorpresa, se ha posesionado demasiado pronto de su papel. Bien. Lo tienen hoy. Que lo gocen mientras sirva a nuestros propósitos. (28)

Samuel, or one like him, will always control the throne. Here, he suggests his control over Saul if the latter should go too far in his role as king. Samuel puts into action his threats implied in this speech. First, he sends the pre-anointed David to Saul just when the king, overcome by the inner conflict between his personal and his public lives, seems to have lost his will to rule. Then, when the relationship between David and Jonathan develops into such a strong love that it becomes a threat to Samuel's power, he uses his political force to destroy that bond.

At the end of the play, Samuel's role is transformed from that of a corrupt judge-priest jealous of those he chooses to serve his purposes, to the personification of the very power that has corrupted him and that continues to corrupt those whom he controls. It is not coincidence that Saul's suicide and the fatal fight between David and Jonathan take place in the same location where Samuel annoited both Saul and David. When, as Jonathan dies, David realizes the significance of what he has done, Samuel suddenly appears "como si surgiera de las entrañas de la tierra" (54) and makes clear his rule:

> Has hecho lo que debías hacer, lo que estaba escrito que harías.
> DAVID.—¿Asesinar . . . el amor?
> SAMUEL.—¡No hay tiempo para el amor! ¡Cesa ya tus lamentaciones! Tú eres el ungido por mí. Tú eres rey. (55)

The play ends as it began with the presence of Samuel, who has traversed more than fifteen years with his power untouched. The presence of this corrupt power always is in the background creating the tension that underlies the personal thoughts and desires of the others, who in the end, are nothing more than puppets.

In the opening scene of *Tito y Berenice*, Tito insists on his love for the Judean princess, while she, at every instance, invokes his role as a Roman citizen. Tito, in vain tries to rid himself of his political identity:

TITO.—No necesito leer un poema de amor hebreo para comprender mis sentimientos.
BERENICE.—¿Los sentimientos de un ciudadano de Roma?
TITO.—(*Altivo.*) No de un ciudadano de Roma, sino de Tito Flavio Vespuciano.
BERENICE.—(*Sonriiendo.*) Heredero al trono imperial, claro está. (65)

He reveals in this dialogue the difficulty he has in ridding himself of that identity. Berenice's reference to him as a citizen, sparks his pride so that he refers to himself by name. His name, however, is what links him most directly to his generational role as the perpetuator of the political power of his father.

The second scene takes place two days prior to the first at the country estate of Herod Agrippa during the fall of Jerusalem to Tito's army and reveals the vindictive nature of the previous scene. Herod demands that his daughter disrobe and declares her beauty to be his instrument of revenge. There is no need for Berenice to resond dramatically at this point to her father's order since we already know that she does go to Tito and he does fall in love with her. Because of the precariousness of their relationship established in these two scenes, the spectator constantly must doubt the authenticity of the feeling of love expressed throughout the rest of the play.

Time as a destructive force is constantly in the background of Tito and Berenice's relationship. There is a significant age difference between them as Berenice is older thanTito by an undisclosed number of years. She mentions his youth in the first scene and associates it with Tito's impulsiveness and lack of experience at living. In the second, Berenice's father emphasizes the fact that his daughter is not a young woman when he says to her: "No estás mal para tu edad" (67). This difference in ages is then related to the conflict of the personal vs. political power when Tito leaves Berenice for Rome:

TITO.—Volveré para llevarte a Roma. Un día volveré, Berenice. Un día volveré. . . .
BERENICE.—Sí, un día volverás . . . Volverás . . . Pero . . . cuán lejos de *mi* tiempo estará *ese* día. (73)

Clearly, the two are heading in different directions as they part. During the rest of the play, Tito is always very much in the public view while Berenice remains a captive princess in her own palace.

Her identity hidden by a veil, she appears before Tito on three occasions during the remainder of the play and becomes the representation of Tito's personal feelings and desires. On the first occasion, she escapes and goes to Rome at Tito's coronation where she appears as a beggar woman. Wearing a purple veil which covers her head and face, she receives Tito's permission to take his hand, he being unaware of her identity. Tito's reaction, while ambiguous, reveals the presence of the conflict. The stage directions read as follows:

> Berenice, alzando a medias su manto, o velo, besa largamente la mano de Tito. Se retira y desaparece entre la multitud, mientras Tito con una expresión dolorosa en su rostro, recoge lentamente su mano derecha y aprieta ésta con la izquierda. No sabemos si es dolor por una mordida o por un beso que ha mordido muy hondo su corazón. . . . (75)

This constitutes the whole action of this short scene, making the impression it leaves with the spectator of Tito's apparent anguish the scene's most important aspect. Because Berenice's identity is actually hidden, Tito appears to *feel* the anguish but does not recognize its source.

The princess' second appearance is again ambiguous. There is nothing in the stage directions that explicitly says the principal dancer in "The Dance of the Veils" is Berenice. Since, again, she is covered by veils and a mask, it is only important that Tito relate her to Berenice. The association comes about mainly because the dancers are Jewish women brought by the Empress to entertain her guests. The mask, however, is the factor that relates this dancer to the Berenice-Tito age relationship for the theatre viewer. According to the author's directions:

> Cuando deja caer el velo total vemos que el cuerpo de la primera bailarina está cubierta por velos transparentes de diversos colores, de los cuales va desprendiéndose, aunque conservará hasta el final el velo sobre su rostro. Ya desnuda, al quitarse este último, aparecerá su rostro con máscara de oro, de facciones femeninas juveniles. (86)

This mask, which Tito picks up after the volcanic eruption, becomes the symbol of his lost love—a symbol conveyed when he brings the mask to his lips and murmurs Berenice's name. The nature itself of a mask, however, is to hide what is beneath. This mask of youthful feminine features, associated with Berenice, immediately calls to mind her age and Tito's denial (conscious or unconscious) of what effect passing time may have had on her once youthful features.

In her last appearance before Tito, she is once again covered by a veil. For the first time since their parting years before, Tito goes to see Berenice. Tito now has the permission of the Senate to take Berenice to Rome as his wife and he naively expects the previous relationship to resume. According to his former lover, however, it is now too late. Tito responds still not understanding: "¿Tarde, cuando tengo en mi poder el mundo?" (98). Berenice, then, must push the Emporer into a revelation by uncovering her withered face. She asks him if he could turn the calendar around. He responds "¿Cambiando el calendario oficial, quieres decir?" (99), still trying to use his power as an answer to the crisis. Berenice's response reveals to him the true reality which he has ignored during their separation—that time has continued to work and her world has not stood still:

> No. Echando atrás horas, días, semanas, meses, años . . . Eliminando, con tu poderosa mano, la áspera labor del tiempo. (99)

As Berenice talks, with her back to Tito, she slowly removes her veil, then turns to him, revealing her aged face and white hair. Tito responds with a look of horror. The same aspects of his personality that made him so vulnerable to the effects of power, make him ignorant of the effects of time until this confrontation.

The element which most clearly links the two plays for the spectator is their identical structure, both internal and external. The cinematic illusion reinforces this similarity as well as the temporal relationship between the two works. On a superficial level, each work contains ten scenes and the two are of approximately the same playing time. Furthermore, they both concern rulers of the Israeli nation—one at the beginning of the monarchy, the other, at its end.

Within the plays' inner structures, an identical pattern prevails as indicated in the single subtitle: "amor, poder, desamor." Each time any authentic feelings of love begin to develop, power in one form or another, appears and destroys love. Indeed, in the second play, power does not merely destroy love, but prevents it from ever fully developing.

In *Sacrificio en el Monte Moriah*, René Marqués captures the spectator's attention through the utilization of cinematographic techniques which he adapts to the theatre. The *montage* and the scenic fluidity together with the dramatization of the familiar Biblical events guide the spectator to concentrate on the theme of sacrifice and violence and encourage him/her to think about this theme in his/her own world of the present. In the twin plays, *David y Jonatán/Tito y*

Berenice, the illusion of cinematic celerity reinforces the temporal significance for the spectator. The works move so quickly and with so many changes that they might be better produced as a film. The dialogue is sketchy and stark with no superfluous details of any kind. Certainly, the illusion of cinema to present two very similar works draws them together as one, leading the spectator to perceive their relationship and his own to the words of the ancient author of Ecclesiastes: "No hay nada de nuevo bajo el sol."

Chapter VIII

Conclusions

When René Marqués proposed the idea of the "Experimental Theatre" to the Ateneo Puertorriqueños's Board of Directors in 1951, he began a career that would immortalize him as an energizing force in the continuing development of Puerto Rican theatre and as an undaunted defender of Puerto Rican culture. Marqués' dedication to the total freedom of the Puerto Rican people in terms of political autonomy as well as individual potential is overwhelmingly obvious in the large majority of his dramatic works. Almost all of his characters suffer a crisis in which their way of life is threatened by some more powerful force, resulting in their struggle to maintain, find or acknowledge their national and individual identity within a culture in great stress. He relates the menacing power, directly or indirectly, to the materialistic consumer society which the United States' presence in every aspect of Puerto Rican life represents for him.

The resolution of these dramatic crises, whether negative or positive, communicates to the theatre public on two levels. First, it points to the injustice of the system portrayed. On another level, it implies the individual's own complicity in the maintenance of that unjust system by virtue of the fact that he/she neither overtly rejects nor accepts it. Marqués' message to the Puerto Rican people, therefore, is a criticism of those people as well, in which he says that one must make some kind of a choice. Non-action always leads to disaster for his characters as he believed it would for his people.

The dynamics of his theatrical composition depend on the particular ways in which he uses time and space to create dramatically the various crises. For example, he combines the elements of real stage space—the set, lights, colors, sounds, props—to create a virtual space whose architectural *ambiance* is at the heart of the crisis dramatized. Every play's virtual space is a form of family living quarters which reflect the conscious or subconscious states-of-mind of the principal characters. These living quarters offer protection from the outside threat and become self-created, escapist worlds which symbolize the self-condemnation of the individuals confined to them. Such confinement prevents physical freedom, related politically to Puerto Rico's commonwealth status with the United States, and personal freedom, related to the development of every human being's creative potential.

Time, in Marqués' plays, serves to heighten the urgency of the major conflicts, becoming at times a powerful villain. The longer the characters procrastinate taking action, the more unrelentlessly time passes until it is transformed into an uncontrollable, life-destroying force. Time manifests itself in various ways in these dramatic works as the author translates temporal elements such as rhythm and tempo, for example, into dramatic devices integrated into the ambiance of the virtual space already mentioned. Marqués also often toys with his audience while he experiments with the presentation of a particular play's linear movement. Frequently he avails himself of the cinematic "flashback" or creates a temporal universality in which past, present, and future meet and even coexist. In addition, history as a record of time, plays a very important role in Marqués' dramatic creations. Sometimes it manifests itself as specific known events and other times it is a fictionalized history. Whether real or created, history always influences the present roles of the characters.

The particular crises are created and/or revealed when any of the aforementioned spatial and temporal elements are integrated with each other. In one of the early plays, *El sol y los MacDonald*, for instance, the past history of the MacDonald house coincides with that of the present generations of the MacDonald family. The bigotry and prejudice of past generations have contributed to the crisis of the present and only the youngest family member is able to escape. The others have waited too long and now cannot change. A similar relationship between space and time is evident in each of the early plays discussed.

Comparable integrations of space and time appear in the later plays and result in crises that are always related to the struggle to maintain one's security through fear vs. the desire for the freedom of dignity and self-respect. In *Un niño azul para esa sombra* and *Los soles truncos*, past, present, and future coexist—in the first case in the innermost consciousness of the child protagonist, Michelín, and in the second, within the family home and interpersonal relationships of the three Burkhart sisters. In these two plays, a final, forced confrontation with the limits of space and time, effectuates the characters' suicide. However, the suicides themselves are neutral actions, while the decisions to finally do something to combat the outside menace are heroic ones.

The crises arising out of *La carreta* and *Carnnaval afuera, carnaval adentro* correspond closely to the concept of rhythm within the created virtual space. In the first, the rhythm begins as a slow, peaceful lifestyle that progressively develops into a fragmented non-rhythmic noise, perhaps best represented by the jackhammer heard at the beginning of the third act. The disintegrating rhythm correlates to the breakdown of the family and the growing distance from their native culture and finally terminates in Luis' death and doña Gabriela and Juanita's decision to return to their native land. Rhythm, in *Carnaval afuera, carnaval adentro* reflects the chaos of Carnival juxtaposed to the tranquility of the tempo which the artist Angel advocates. This rhythmic conflict itself is mirrored in the characters' speeches and actions and in the space which they occupy. The title indicates that the conflict is also a spatial one, with the "outside" being the actual Carnival Festival taking place in which participants are masked, while the "inside" refers to the individual's disguising of his/her true inner motivations, resulting in hypocrisy. Both plays end in a death. In the case of Luis in *La carreta*, he is responsible for his own end because of his stubbornness in adhering to foreign ways. In *Carnaval afuera, carnaval adentro*, the characters never give up their hypocrisy and in the end collectively assassinate Rosie, who represents their innocence.

The historical space of the past plays the key role in *La muerte no entrará en palacio* and *Mariana o el alba*. The first of these two plays surrounds the dramatization of Governor Muñoz Marín's signing of the Commonwealth agreement with an aura of myth and immortality. The well-known events, however, are changed by the murder of the famous and popular governer before he signs the agreement; thus, immortality is granted to the murderer who is, in the dramatization, his daughter. The play takes place on the terrace of the governor's mansion, a famous, historical building called "La Fortaleza" in present-day Puerto Rico and "El palacio" in the play. Gradually, the governor's movement towards the signing of the agreement transforms the palace into a figurative prison from which those who live inside are afraid to leave. When the governor's assassination occurs in this famous space just prior to his signing of the agreement, the audience is left to cope with the change in historical reality.

Mariana o el alba treats history in a slightly different way. The history re-created here is as faithful in every detail as possible but, in this case, the space and even the detailed events are unfamiliar to the audience (or were at the play's writing). Time affects the historic events dramatized through waiting. First, the characters wait for the unsuccessful revolution and the stillborn child. At play's end, the audience finds itself left waiting, still for the revolution. The spectators also are implicated in initiating the unfulfilled revolution since the play's heroes cannot, by virtue of their being historical figures from the previous century. In this way, past, present, and future are actually fused into the virtual historical space created on the stage.

The last three plays that Marqués wrote, *Sacrificio en el Monte Moriah*, and *David y Jonatán/Tito y Berenice,* treat space and time in a much different way than any of the others, but the crises themselves depict a pattern comparable to those of the previous plays. The times and spaces dramatized obviously are from a remote Biblical past and only the stories themselves are familiar. Marqués presents his stories through the illusions created by cinematic techniques. In this way, he eliminates (or nearly so) the spatial and temporal limits which the stage would ordinarily impose. *Sacrificio en el Monte Moriah* presents the conflict between Abraham's thirst for material comforts and power at the cost of the victimization of Sara and her son Isaac. The action shifts back and forth between the remote past to one even more remote to dramatize the motivation for Sara's final act of violence. The fourteen scenes shift back and forth between one stage space and another by the use of platforms and lights, creating the illusion of the kind of fast-moving montage one expects from the cinema but not from the stage. All of this forces the attention of the spectator on the events dramatized more so than on the elements of real stage space and real time, making the message more explicit than ever.

The same can be said of the twin plays *David y Jonatán/Tito y Berenice* which the author requested be published and produced as one. The dynamic element of time in these plays, aside from the cinematic celerity parallel to that of *Sacrificio,* is the "flashback." Events are produced in short impressionistic scenes with very few details and the stage sets are for the most part simple by necessity since there are so many rapid changes. The flashbacks provide the motives for scenes previously portrayed and leave the spectator to fill in the missing details. Moreover, because the two plays take place in Biblical times and concern the Jewish people, time and space are the factors that tie the works together as well as imply their relevance to the present world.

In view of the analogous patterns evident in the body of René Marqués' dramatic works, it is appropriate to relate those patterns to his own circumstances. Marqués offers as an epigraph to his panto-mimed ballet, *Juan Bobo y la Dama de Occidente,* the following quote from Ortega y Gasset's *Meditaciones del Quijote:* Yo soy yo y mi circunstancia, y si no la salvo a ella no me salvo yo" (13). This quotation became the motto for all of his works. The confined spaces of his plays are analogous to his own living space on a small island between the Atlantic Ocean and the Caribbean Sea. While the seas might offer unlimited freedom such as that which he advocates, the political relationship between Puerto Rico and the United States prevents the Island's unique potential from developing fully. In a similar way, the materialism Marqués associates with the United States adversely affects both the people of his homeland and his characters.

Time, in his plays, imitate first the fusion of the past with the present so obvious in many places on the Island because of the juxtaposition of historical buildings and sites to contemporary ones. Furthermore, the rhythms established in several of the works imitate that of the consumer society portrayed as a threat to the survival of the Puerto Rican culture. The passage of time—always the villain— would seem to indicate that while the people wait and do not take a stand, time runs out until actions may come too late.

These interpretations may be true or not. What is certain, however, is that René Marqués, sincerely dedicated to the well-being of his people and his land, was and through his works, continues to be, one of the great dramatists of the twentieth century.

Works Cited

Abel, Lionel. *Metatheatre: A New View of Dramatic Form.* New York: Hill and Wang, 1963.

Actas Oficiales del Ateneo Puertorriqueño. (el 13 de octubre de 1930), Vol. 7:n.p.

—. (el 29 de diciembre de 1938), Vol. 8:n.p.

Arce de Vázquez, Margot. "*La carreta* de René Marqués." *El Mundo* el 24 de octubre de 1953, 6.

Arriví, Francisco. " ' El Apartamiento' de René Marqués." *El Mundo,* Suplemento Sabatino el 11 de abril de 1964, 10.

—. *Areyto mayor.* San Juan, Puerto Rico: Instituto de Cultura Puertorriqueña, 1966.

Aylen, Leo. *Greek Tragedy and the Modern World.* London: Methuen and Co., Ltd., 1964.

Babín, María Teresa. "Apuntes sobre *La carreta. La carreta.* 12a ed. Río Piedras, Puerto Rico: Editorial Cultural, Inc., 1975, v-xxi.

Bazin,André. "The Evolution of the Language of Cinema." *Film Theory and Criticism.* Eds. Gerald Mast and Marshall Cohen, 2d ed. London: Oxford University Press, 1979, 123-139.

Belaval, Emilio. "El Club Artístico de Puerto Rico." *El Mundo* el 17 de marzo de 1958: Page number unreadable; and el 26 de marzo de 1958, 14.

—. "Lo que podría ser un teatro puertorriqueño." 1939. *Areyto mayor* de Francisco Arriví. Appendix 1. San Juan, Puerto Rico: Instituto de Cultura Puertorriquña, 1966, 245-258.

Belázs, Béla. "The Face of Man." *Film Theory and Criticism.* Eds. Gerald Mast and Marshall Cohen, 2d ed. London: Oxford University Press, 1979, 290-298.

Cuchi Coll, Isabel. " 'El Apartamiento': Segunda obra de Séptimo Festival de Teatro." *El Imparcial,* Sabatino el 11 de abril de 1964, S-4, S-18.

Dauster, Frank. "Frye and Fergusson: Hacia una teoría del teatro." *Texto Crítico.*

Año V. 15 (Octubre a diciembre de 1979), 128-132.

—. *Historia del teatro hispanoamericano, Siglos XIX y XX.* 2a ed. Mexico: Ediciones De Andrea, 1973.

—. "New Plays of René Marqués." *Hispania.* September 1960, XLIII,3:451-452.

—. "René Marqués y el tiempo culpable." *Ensayos sobre teatro hispanoamericano.* México: SepSetentas, 1975, 102-126.

—. "The Theatre of René Marqués." *Symposium.* Spring, 1964, XVIII,1:35-45.

Espinosa, Victoria. "*El apartamiento.*" *Homenaje a René Marqués: XVI Festival de Teatro 1982.* San Juan, Puerto Rico: Ateneo Puertorriqueño, 1982, 34.

Feeny, Thomas. "Woman's Triumph over Man in René Marqués' Theatre." *Hispania.* May 1982, 65,2:187-193.

Fernández, Dr. Piri. "Temas del teatro puertorriqueño." *El autor dramático.* San Juan, Puerto Rico: Instituto de Cultura Puertorriqueña, 1963, 153-182. Primer Seminario de Dramaturgia.

Fraser, Howard M. "Theatricality in *The Fanlights* and *Payment as Pledged.* *The American Hispanist.* September, 1977, XIX,3:6-8.

González, Nilda. *Bibliografía de Teatro Puertorriqueño: Siglos XIX y XX.* Río Piedras, Puerto Rico: Editorial Universitaria, 1979.

Holzapfel, Tamara. "The Theater of René Marqués: In Search of Identity and Form." *Dramatists in Revolt: The New Latin American Theater.* Eds. Leon F. Lyday and George W. Woodyard. Austin, Texas: University of Texas Press, 1976, 146-166.

Kracauer, Siegfried. "The Establishment of Physical Existence." *Film Theory and Criticism.* Eds. Gerald Mast and Marshall Cohen, 2d ed. London: Oxford University Press, 1979, 264-278.

Lacomba, José. Personal interview. Spring, 1982.

—. "René Marqués: The Man and the Dramatist." Unpublished ms. N.p.: n.p., n.d.

Langer, Susanne K. *Feeling and Form: A Theory of Art.* New York: Charles Scribner's Sons, 1953.

Lyday, Leon F. and George W. Woodyard. *A Bibliography of Latin American Theater Criticism: 1940-1970.* Austin, Texas: University of Texas Press, 1976.

Maldonado Denis, Manuel. *Mito y realidad.* 3a ed. Río Piedras, Puerto Rico: Editorial Antillana, 1979.

Marqués, René. *El apartamiento. Teatro*. Tomo III. Río Piedras, Puerto Rico: Editorial Cultural, Inc., 1971, 107-207.

—. *Carnaval adentro, carnaval afuera*. Río Piedras, Puerto Rico: Editorial Cultural, Inc., 1971.

—. *La carreta*. 12a ed. Río Piedras, Puerto Rico: Editorial Cultural, Inc., 1975.

—. *La casa sin reloj. Teatro*. Tomo III. Río Piedras, Puerto Rico: Editorial Cultural, Inc., 1971, 11-106.

—. *Los condenados*. Unpublished ms. 1951.

—. *David y Jonatán. Tito y Berenice. Dos dramas de amor, poder y desamor*. Río Piedras, Puerto Rico: Editorial Antillana, 1970.

—. *En una ciudad llamada San Juan*. 5a ed. Río Piedras, Puerto Rico: Editorial Cultural, 1983.

—. "El Estreno de Esta Noche: *La Casa Sin Reloj*." *El Mundo* el 28 de sept. de 1961, 10.

—. *El hombre y sus sueños. Teatro*. Tomo II. Río Piedras, Puerto Rico: Editorial Cultural, Inc., 1971, 13-49.

—. "Luigi Pirandello: *El Hombre ante su Espejo*." *Asomante*. oct-dic 1967, XXIII,4:27-31.

—. *Mariana o el alba*. Edición Centenaria del Grito de Lares. Río Piedras, Puerto Rico: Editorial Antillana, 1968.

—. *La muerte no entrará en palacio. Teatro*. Tomo 1. 2a ed. Río Piedras, Puerto Rico: Editorial Cultural, Inc., 1970, 182-325.

—. *Un niño azul para esa sombra. Teatro*. Tomo 1. 2a ed. Río Piedras, Puerto Rico: Editorial Cultural, Inc., 1970, 67-181.

—. *Palm Sunday*. Unpublished ms. 1949.

—. "O'Neill, Eugene. *A Moon for the Misbegotten*, Random House, New York, 1952." *Asomante*. 1953, IX,2:91-95.

—. "Usigli, Rodolfo. *Corona de sombra*." *Asomante*. 1948, IV,1:97-100.

—. *Sacrificio en el Monte Moriah*. Río Piedras, Puerto Rico: Editorial Antillana, 1969.

—. *El sol y los MacDonald*. Río Piedras, Puerto Rico: Editorial Cultural, Inc., 1971.

—. *Los soles truncos. Teatro*. Tomo I. 2a ed. Río Piedras, Puerto Rico: Editorial Cultural, Inc., 1970, 5-66.

Martin, Eleanor J. *René Marqués*. Boston: Twayne, 1979.

Morfi, Angelina. "*El Apartamiento:* Nueva Ruta en el Teatro de René Marqués." *El Mundo* el 25 mayo de 1964, 27.

—. *Historia crítica de un Siglo de Teatro Puertorriqueño*. San Juan, Puerto Rico: Instituto de Cultura Puertorriqueña, 1980.

Pasarell, Emilio J. *Orígenes y desarrollo de la afición teatral en Puerto Rico*. 2a. ed. revisada. Partes I y II. Santurce, Puerto Rico: Departamento de Instrucción Pública del Estado Libre Asociado de Puerto Rico, 1969.

Pilditch, Charles. *René Marqués: A Study of His Fiction*. New York: Plus Ultra Educational Publishers Inc., 1976.

Rivera de Alvarez, Josefina. *Diccionario de Literatura Puertorriqueña*. Tomo Segundo. Vols. I & II. 1974. San Juan, Puerto Rico: Instituto de Cultura Puertorriqueña.

Rodríguez Ramos, Esther. "Aproximación a una Bibliografía de René Marqués." *Sin Nombre*. oct-nov 1979, X,3:121-148.

Sánchez, Luis Rafael. "Cinco problemas al escritor puertorriqueño." *Vórtice*. 2.3 N.d., 117-121.

Santos Silva, Loreina. "Reflexiones sobre *Los soles truncos* de René Marqués." *Ceiba*. II.3 jul-dic. 1973, 63-67.

Sartre, Jean Paul. *Being and Nothingness*. Trans. Hazel E. Barnes. New York: The Citadel Press, 1964.

Siemens, William L. "Assault on the Schizoid Wasteland: René Marqués' *El apartamiento*." *Latin American Theatre Review*. Spring 1974, 7,2:17-23.

Shaw, Donald L. "René Marqués' *La muerte no entrará en palacio*: An Analysis." *Latin American Theatre Review*, Fall 1968, 2,1:31-38.

Smiley, Sam. *Playwriting: The Structure of Action*. Englewood Cliffs, New Jersey: Prentice-Hall, Inc., 1971.

Solórzano, Carlos. *Teatro latinoamericano en el siglo XX*. Mexico: Editorial Pormaca, S.A. de c.v., 1964.

Sontag, Susan. "Film and Theatre." *Film Theory and Criticism*. Eds. Gerald Mast and Marshall Cohen, 2d ed. London: Oxford University Press, 1979, 359-377.

Styan, J. L. *Drama, Stage and Audience*. New York: Cambridge University Press, 1975.

—. *The Elements of Drama*. New York: Cambridge University Press, 1963.

Vázquez, Alamo F. "Análisis prologal." *David y Jonatán. Tito y Berenice.* Río Piedras, Puerto Rico: Editorial Antillana, 1970, 7-13.

Villegas, Juan. *Interpretación y análisis del texto dramático.* Primera ed. Colección Telón. Ottawa, Ontario: Girol Books, Inc., 1982.

Webster's New Collegiate Dictionary. Springfield, MS: G. & C., MerriamCo., 1973.

Zalacaín, Daniel. "René Marqués, del absurdo a la realidad." *Latin American Theatre Review,* Fall 1978, 12,1:33-37.